Introduction

Welcome to LifeLight

A special pleasure is in store for you. You will be instrumental in leading your brothers and sisters in Christ closer to Him who is our life and light (John 1:4). You will have the pleasure of seeing fellow Christians discover new insights and rediscover old ones as they open the Scriptures and dig deep into them, perhaps deeper than they have ever dug before. More than that, you will have the pleasure of sharing in this wonderful study.

LifeLight—An In-depth Study

LifeLight is a series of in-depth Bible studies. The goal of LifeLight is that through a regular program of in-depth personal and group study of Scripture, more and more Christian adults may grow in their personal faith in Jesus Christ, enjoy fellowship with the members of His body, and reach out in love to others in witness and service.

In-depth means that this Bible study includes the following four components: individual daily home study; discussion in a small group; a lecture presentation on the Scripture portion under study; and an enhancement of the week's material (through reading the enrichment magazine).

LifeLight Participants

LifeLight participants are adults who desire a deeper study of the Scriptures than is available in the typical Sunday morning adult Bible class. (Mid-to-older teens might also be LifeLight participants.) While LifeLight does not assume an existing knowledge of the Bible or special experience or skills in Bible study, it does assume a level of commitment that will bring participants to each of the nine weekly assemblies having read the assigned readings and attempted to answer the study questions. Daily reading and study will require from 15 to 30 minutes for the five days preceding the LifeLight assembly. The day following the assembly will be spent reviewing the previous week's study by going over the completed study leaflet and the enrichment magazine.

LifeLight Leadership

While the in-depth process used by LifeLight begins with individual study and cannot achieve its aims without this individual effort, it cannot be completed by individual study alone. Therefore, trained leaders are necessary. You fill one or perhaps more of the important roles described below.

The Director

This person oversees the LifeLight program in a local center (which may be a congregation or a center operated by several neighboring congregations). The director

- serves as the parish LifeLight overall coordinator and leader;
- coordinates the scheduling of the LifeLight program;
- orders materials;
- convenes LifeLight leadership team meetings;
- develops publicity materials;
- recruits participants;
- maintains records and budgeting;
- assigns, with the leadership team, participants to small discussion groups;
- makes arrangements for facilities;
- communicates outreach opportunities to small-group leaders and to congregational boards;
- follows up on participants who leave the program.

The Assistant Director *(optional)*

This person may assist the director. Duties listed for the director may be assigned to the assistant director as mutually agreeable.

The Lecture Leader

This person prepares and delivers the lecture at the weekly assembly. **(Lesson material for the lecture leader begins on p. 9.)** The lecture leader

- prepares and presents the Bible study lecture to the large group;
- prepares worship activities (devotional thought, hymn, prayer), using resources in the study leaflet and leaders guide and possibly other outside sources;
- helps the small-group discussion leaders to grow in understanding the content of the lessons;
- encourages prayer at weekly leadership team and discussion leaders meetings.

The Small-Group Coordinator *(optional; the director may fill this role)*

This person supervises and coordinates the work of the small-group discussion leaders. The small-group coordinator

- recruits with the leadership team the small-group discussion leaders;
- trains or arranges for training of the discussion leaders;
- assists the director and discussion leaders in follow-up and outreach;
- encourages the discussion leaders to contact absent group members;
- participates in the weekly leadership-team and discussion-leaders equipping meetings;
- provides ongoing training and support as needed.

The Small-Group Discussion Leaders

These people guide and facilitate discussion of LifeLight participants in the small groups. **(Lesson material for the small-group leaders begins on p. 51.)** There should be one discussion leader for every group of no more than twelve participants. The small-group discussion leaders are, perhaps, those individuals who are most important to the success of the program. They should, therefore, be chosen with special care and be equipped with skills needed to guide discussion and to foster a caring fellowship within the group. These discussion leaders

- prepare each week for the small-group discussion by using the study leaflet and small-group leaders guide section for that session **(see p. 51)**;
- read the enrichment magazine as a study supplement;
- guide and facilitate discussion in their small group;
- encourage and assist the discussion group in prayer;
- foster fellowship and mutual care within the discussion group;
- attend weekly discussion-leaders training meetings.

Leadership Training

LifeLight leaders will meet weekly to review the previous week's work and plan the coming week. At this session, leaders can address concerns and prepare for the coming session. LifeLight is a 1½-hour program with no possibility for it to be taught in the one hour typically available on Sunday mornings. Some congregations, however, may want to use the Sunday morning Bible study hour for LifeLight preparation and leadership training. In such a meeting, the lecture leader and/or small-group coordinator may lead the discussion leaders through the coming week's lesson, reserving 5 or 10 minutes for problem solving or other group concerns.

While it requires intense effort, LifeLight has proven to bring great benefit to LifeLight participants. The effort put into this program, both by leaders and by participants, will be rewarding and profitable.

The LifeLight Weekly Schedule

Here is how LifeLight will work week by week:

1. Before session 1, each participant will receive the study leaflet for session 1 and the enrichment magazine for the course. The study leaflet contains worship resources (for use both in individual daily study and at the opening of the following week's assembly) and readings and study questions for five days. Challenge questions will lead those participants who have the time and desire a greater challenge into even deeper levels of study.
2. After the five days of individual study at home, participants will gather for a weekly assembly of all LifeLight participants. The assembly will begin with a brief period of worship (5 minutes). Participants will then join their assigned small discussion groups (of twelve or fewer, who will remain the same throughout the course), where they will go over the week's

LifeLight

"In Him was life, and the life was the light of men." John 1:4

Isaiah, Part 1

LEADERS GUIDE

CONCORDIA PUBLISHING HOUSE • SAINT LOUIS

An angel reached out with a burning coal, touched Isaiah's mouth, and said: "Behold . . . your guilt is taken away, and your sin atoned for" (Isaiah 6:7). What Isaiah experienced that day must have both shocked and thrilled him. In the presence of the Holy One of Israel, he learned about his sin and also about the atonement for sin that only the Lord can provide. As you study Isaiah's prophecies you, too, will be touched and thrilled by the Lord's Word for you.

Copyright ©1994, 2006 by Concordia Publishing House
3558 S. Jefferson Ave.
St. Louis, MO 63118-3968

1-800-325-3040 • cph.org

All rights reserved. No part of this publication may be reproduced, stored in a retrieval system, or transmitted, in any form or by any means, electronic, mechanical, photocopying, recording, or otherwise, without the prior written permission of Concordia Publishing House.

Edward Engelbrecht, editor

Revised from material by Andrew H. Bartelt and Jane Fryar; contributions by Edward Engelbrecht

Denise Muhly, Lavern Schmidt, and Rick Gallagher, field-test coordinators

LifeLight field-test sites: St. Peter Lutheran Church, Lodi, CA—Rev. Zimmermann, Pastor; Bethlehem Lutheran Church, Lakewood, CO—Rev. Dyer, pastor.

Developed under the auspices of the LifeLight Committee of The Lutheran Church—Missouri Synod, with funding assistance from the International Lutheran Women's Missionary League.

Scripture quotations are from The Holy Bible, English Standard Version, copyright © 2001 by Crossway Bibles, a division of Good News Publishers. Used by permission. All rights reserved.

Logo quotation and other Scripture quotations marked NIV are taken from the HOLY BIBLE, NEW INTERNATIONAL VERSION®. NIV®. Copyright © 1973, 1978, 1984 by International Bible Society. Used by permission of Zondervan Publishing House. All rights reserved.

Scripture quotations marked NKJV are taken from the New King James Version. Copyright © 1979, 1980, 1982 by Thomas Nelson, Inc. Used by permission. All rights reserved.

This publication may be available in braille, in large print, or on cassette tape for the visually impaired. Please allow 8 to 12 weeks for delivery. Write to the Library for the Blind, 7550 Watson Rd., St. Louis, MO 63119-4409; call toll-free 1-888-215-2455; or visit the Web site: www.blindmission.org.

Cover illustration: Richard Hook

Manufactured in the U.S.A.

3 4 5 6 7 8 9   29 28 27 26 25 24

Contents

study questions together (55 minutes). Assembling together once again, participants will listen to a lecture presentation on the readings they have studied in the previous week and discussed in their small groups (20 minutes). After the lecture presentation, the director or another leader will distribute the study leaflet for the following week. Closing announcements and other necessary business may take another five minutes before dismissal.

In some places some small groups will not join the weekly assembly because of scheduling or other reasons. Such groups may meet at another time and place (perhaps in the home of one of the small group's members). Those congregations may record the lecture given by the lecture leader at the weekly assembly and duplicate it for use by other groups meeting later in the week.

3. On the day following the assembly, participants will review the preceding week's work by rereading the study leaflet they completed (and that they perhaps supplemented or corrected during the discussion in their small group) and by reading appropriate articles in the enrichment magazine.

Then the LifeLight weekly study process will begin all over again!

Recommended Study Resources for Isaiah

Concordia Self-Study Bible, New International Version. St. Louis: Concordia Publishing House, 1986. Interpretive notes on each page form a running commentary on the text. The book includes cross-references, a 35,000-word concordance, full-color maps, charts, and timelines.

Delitzsch, Franz. *Biblical Commentary on the Prophecies of Isaiah.* Grand Rapids: Wm. B. Eerdmans Co., 1973. An important classic resource.

Keil, C. F. and Franz Delitzsch. *Isaiah–A Biblical Commentary on the Old Testament.* Grand Rapids: Wm. B. Eerdmans Publishing Co., 1971. A standard Old Testament commentary by two outstanding conservative scholars. A careful study of the original text and its implications for biblical theology. Although somewhat old, it is still a helpful resource.

Leupold, Herbert C. *An Exposition of Isaiah.* Grand Rapids: Baker, 1977. A careful exposition of Isaiah and its messianic prophecies.

Roehrs, Walter R., and Martin H. Franzmann. *Concordia Self-Study Commentary.* St. Louis: Concordia Publishing House, 1979. This one-volume commentary on the Bible is tailored for lay use.

Young, Edward J. *The Book of Isaiah.* Grand Rapids: Wm. B. Eerdmans Publishing Co., 1992. The magnum opus of a great conservative scholar. Carefully interprets the many prophecies of Isaiah in their context; also stresses their messianic import.

Every Voice a Song: Pipe Organ Accompaniment for 180 Hymns and Liturgy. St. Louis: Concordia Publishing House (order no. 99-1565). Use this music CD for worship hymn accompaniment.

Isaiah, Mighty Seer

Isaiah 1, 6, and Related Historical Texts

Preparing for the Session

Central Focus

As we begin this study of Isaiah, we meet its author. We set the social, political, and spiritual stage for the Book as we probe conditions in the nation of Judah in the seventh century before Christ. We also catch a glimpse of God's glory as He reveals Himself to Isaiah and calls him into the prophetic office.

Objectives

That the participant, led by the Holy Spirit through the Word, will

1. understand the political, social, and spiritual scene into which God sent Isaiah as His spokesman;
2. comprehend Isaiah's message as one of both sin and grace, Law and Gospel;
3. realize that the message of repentance and forgiveness that Isaiah spoke to God's Old Testament people is the same message our Lord speaks to us today;
4. respond to that message in humble confession and confident peace, assured that his or her sins are forgiven for Jesus' sake.

Note for the small-group leaders: Lesson notes and other materials you will need begin on page 51.

For the Lecture Leader

Session Plan

Worship

Begin the session with the hymn and the prayer printed in the study leaflet. Hymn accompaniments are available in denominational hymnals, such as *Lutheran Worship* (*LW*, refer to hymnal index). (Note: Concordia Publishing House has available *Every Voice a Song*, a 9-CD set of organ accompaniments for 180 hymns and liturgy. All the initial worship hymns in the LifeLight courses are included in this resource. It's especially helpful for mission congregations and small parishes. See the list of study resources on page 7.)

Lecture Presentation

Introduction

In the year that John Kennedy died . . .

On the morning the space shuttle Challenger exploded . . .

On the day the towers fell . . .

Do you recall significant times in your life by linking them with historical events like these, especially with traumatic ones? If so, you'll more likely understand the shudder that shook the hearts of the people of Judah as they heard these words from Isaiah's lips: "In the year that King Uzziah died . . ." (Isaiah 6:1).

1 In the Year King Uzziah Died

We receive a full account of the events from 2 Chronicles 26. Uzziah's fifty-two-year reign was marked by prosperity and national accomplishment. What an administrator! The people of Judah benefited from Uzziah's various national programs. His ambitious building projects fostered national pride, as well as boosted the economy. Uzziah's agricultural policies no doubt ensured a plentiful food supply and put many unskilled laborers to work. Even Uzziah's military exploits to the west and south probably proved popular. For one thing, Judah reclaimed territory from its glory days. For another, the tribute Uzziah extorted from those he defeated in battle would have helped lower the tax rate at home. Flags flew high in Judah as long as Uzziah sat on David's throne.

But prosperity has its hazards, hazards perhaps more treacherous than adversity. We may let down our guard. We may forget the dangers we face, dangers from without and within. We tend to lose touch with the conditions of the heart. Isaiah reminds us that this subtle hazard has proven deadly time and again throughout history for kings, as well as for us more common folk.

2 Uzziah's Fall

When Isaiah was growing up, Judah was rising up under Uzziah's leadership. Uzziah had fifty-two years on the throne—twelve years more than David or Solomon. Hearts and flags soared in Judah, and Uzziah began to believe his own publicity. While the sixteen-year-old Uzziah "did what was right in the eyes of the LORD according to all that his father Amaziah had done," (2 Chronicles 26:4), the prosperity the Lord gave Judah during Uzziah's reign awakened tragic pride inside the king's heart.

In 2 Chronicles 26, we learn that during the latter years of his reign, Uzziah turned his attention more and more to concerns of military might and prosperity, while his heart grew spiritually numb.

The Scriptures tell us (2 Chronicles 26:16), "But when he was strong, he grew proud, to his destruction. For he was unfaithful to the LORD his God and entered the temple of the LORD to burn incense on the altar of incense."

Uzziah thought himself invincible. He thought himself above the law, even God's law. After all, he may have reasoned, why would a wise and accomplished ruler such as himself need a lowly priest to represent him before God's throne? Who would deny an accomplished ruler access to the temple and its altar? Why shouldn't a king who commanded so much political power also wield a measure of spiritual authority as well?

The king took a censer and bullied his way into the Holy Place of the temple to burn incense. Rebuked by Azariah and eighty other courageous priests who dared to stand up to him, Uzziah became enraged. Impenitent and furious, Uzziah suddenly found himself struck with leprosy. He rushed out of the temple, spurred on by the priests. For the rest of his earthly life, he suffered the lonely consequences of his scheme to grab more honor and power for himself.

3 Assyria—A New Superpower

Isaiah begins with Uzziah's death. The people of Judah were probably fearful and insecure. During Uzziah's fifty-two-year reign, the nations had undergone drastic change. Most notable was the rise of Assyria, the new superpower of that era.

The approach Assyria took to warfare permanently changed the balance of power in the area and chilled the hearts of everyone who lived within striking distance.

Until then, enemy armies would march to the borders of a weaker kingdom, threaten that kingdom's ruler, and demand tribute. Those who were able or willing to pay escaped harm. Those who could not afford to pay the tribute or who thought they could defeat the attacking enemy would march off to war to defend their right to keep their wealth.

The Assyrians changed all that. They put a program of permanent conquest in place. They would round up the populations they defeated and herd nearly all the people off for permanent resettlement in another part of their far-flung empire. Then they would import other captives to resettle the conquered territory. By uprooting the people they conquered, they put an end to rebellion.

How frightening it must have been for the Judeans to face the possible loss of their homes, culture, and perhaps even their language and identity as a people! Imagine yourself being captured by an invading army and then resettled in a village somewhere in the heart of Afghanistan. Imagine that neither you nor the members of your family would ever go home again. In Isaiah's day, the people of Judah found themselves facing that very kind of threat.

Uzziah, the king and Judah's protector, was dead. In 2 Chronicles 27, we learn that Jotham, a young man with an unimpressive track record, had officially ascended to the throne of David. The nation's future looked rocky at best. At least, that's the way the people of Judah must have seen it. But it wasn't the way the Lord saw it. And it wasn't the way He wanted His people to see it either.

4 Isaiah—Mighty Seer

Enter Isaiah, Isaiah the seer, the prophet who by God's grace saw the true dangers Judah faced, and who saw the sins of the past, the spiritual dry rot of the present, and the judgment on the horizon.

In Isaiah 6:1, we learn that in the year King Uzziah died, Isaiah saw the King—the ruler of heaven and earth—high and lifted up. Not King Uzziah, but Yahweh, the Lord. The train of His royal robes filled the temple.

We know from Exodus 33:20 that "man shall not see Me [the Lord] and live." Isaiah says that he saw the Lord. But note well that Isaiah never describes the Lord. Instead, He describes the evidences of the Lord's presence. He focuses especially on the seraphs surrounding the throne that correspond with the "living creatures" mentioned in St. John's vision of heaven (Revelation 4:6–9). In that revelation, as here, each of these angelic beings had six wings. With two wings they flew. Two wings covered their faces in their awe of the divine glory. Two wings covered their feet in their consciousness of the depth at which creatures stand below their great Creator.

King Uzziah had died, but Judah's heavenly King was alive and well. His people were alive also, alive but sick (Isaiah 1:5–6): "The whole head is injured, and the whole heart faint. From the sole of your foot even to the head, there is no soundness in it, but bruises and sores and raw wounds; they are not pressed out or bound up or softened with oil."

Face-to-face with the Holy One of Israel, Isaiah felt the searing shame of his own sinfulness. He cries out in anguish (6:5), "Woe is me! For I am lost; for I am a man of unclean lips, and I dwell in the midst of a people of unclean lips; for my eyes have seen the King, the LORD of hosts!"

"I could have died," we sometimes say. We usually say it as we try to express deep embarrassment over some incident or another. "I could have died."

In that moment, Isaiah the seer could have died. He saw himself in the blinding light of God's holiness. He saw his people in that same blinding light. He saw the reality of his sin, and he fully expected to die from the encounter.

When was the last time we truly felt that way as we approached our holy God with our sins? When was the last time we found ourselves face-to-face with our guilt and the penalty our heavenly King could rightly demand that we pay? When was the last time we really saw the wretched self-centeredness and nauseating infection of the sin that churns inside our own hearts?

Isaiah saw that the words of his lips did not match the actions of his life. He realized that he personally had contributed to the hypocrisy of his outwardly religious but inwardly self-righteous society. Isaiah recognized the futility of trying to make up for his sin by performing a few outward rituals each time he went to church. But the most painful thing of all that Isaiah saw that day was the truth that he personally deserved all the judgment His righteous King could dispense.

It was at that point that Isaiah the seer saw something else (6:6), something wonderful. He saw one of the seraphim—one of the angels whose name means "the burning ones"—fly to the altar and remove from it a burning coal. Isaiah watched the seraph fly to the place in the temple where he stood and with that white-hot coal touch his lips.

As the seraph did that, Isaiah the seer heard. He heard the strong Word of the Lord (6:7): "Behold, this has touched your lips; your guilt is taken away, and your sin atoned for."

The words spoken by our pastors in worship parallel what happened to our brother Isaiah as he stood in the presence of the seraphim that day. We, too, stand before a holy God. We stand there as His forgiven and dearly loved children. How fantastic is that forgiveness! Lord, let us see Your mercy more and more fully, just as You enabled Isaiah to see it.

Then God spoke again (6:8). This time He spoke an invitation and a challenge: "Whom shall I send, and who will go for Us?"

Did you catch it? Do you hear in the "Us" the invitation of the Holy Trinity? God approached Isaiah to ask—not command, but to ask—him to take on the role of ambassador for heaven's King. The psalmist says (Psalm 18:35) of our Lord, "Your gentleness made me great." In His gentleness, the Lord asks, "Whom shall I send?"

Isaiah 6:9–12 requires special comment. In verse 9, the Lord calls the people "this people," not "My people."

They have ceased listening to Him, and He is separating Himself from them. Isaiah's message will deepen the separation. He will dull their eyes, ears, and all their senses in order that they might continue toward destruction. Notice the poetry of verse 10. The Lord comments on their hearts, ears, and eyes. Then He reverses the order to eyes, ears, and hearts (an example of chiasm). The Lord begins with their hearts and ends with their hearts. Their hearts are the problem. The Hebrew term translated "dull" or "calloused" literally means "fat." Their hearts are fat with contentment so that they will not hear and see the truth.

Take note, hearers and readers! As you study Isaiah's prophecies over the coming weeks, do not close your eyes and ears. That temptation will arise as the prophet continually focuses on the Assyrians and Babylonians and repeats his message about the lack of repentance in Israel. Your mind may wander, and your heart may wonder, "What does all this Old Testament history have to do with me?" Exercise your hearts with careful study of the text. See with Isaiah's eyes, and hear with his ears lest your hearts grow dull and fat.

5 Isaiah's Task

Isaiah's assignment would not be easy. None of God's prophets slept in a bed of roses. Like other prophets, Isaiah would speak a hard word. He would point his long, bony finger at the people's sins. He would name names. He would warn and confront. After a while, people would cross the street when they saw him coming. Eventually, if tradition tells the truth, his own people would saw him in half.

From the world's point of view, this prophet, like most of God's Old Testament prophets, was, quite frankly, a nobody. We know little about Isaiah. He mentions his father, wife, and two children in his Book. That's about it as far as our background information goes. All we have is his message. He spoke for Yahweh, the Lord, the King in whose presence the angels veil their faces. Isaiah spoke the Word of the Lord to a people who needed so badly to hear it.

Isaiah spoke of human sin and the judgment the King of kings would rightly impose on those who did not repent. But Isaiah also spoke of a time when Yahweh Himself would come as King, Deliverer, and Savior.

But we're getting ahead of the story. For now, we're stuck with King Jotham and his spiritually sick, impenitent subjects.

Chapter 1 paints a somber picture, a picture rendered in the grays and deep purples of grief. We see the holy, heavenly King crying tears over the rebellion of His people. God's heart aches.

Isaiah 1:3 summarizes the seriousness of the problem. A barnyard animal as ignorant as an ox knows its master, the person who feeds, waters, and cares for it. A donkey at least knows its manger and where to come for food each night. But Israel? Israel knows . . . knows . . . what? The Hebrew sentence simply ends. It ends without a direct object to complete the thought of the verb. Israel knows . . . nothing. As we might say today, Israel just doesn't get it.

In verses 13 and following, the Lord throws up His hands in disgust. "Bring no more vain offerings," He shouts. "Stop trying to appease Me with meaningless rituals! Stop tracking mud across the floor of My holy temple and thinking that I'm pleased that you've come to pray to Me! Your hands drip with the blood of those you've hurt. Your worship services reek with the stench of the lovelessness in your lives. Stop being religious and start being righteous!"

Still, even in judgment, Yahweh longs to show mercy to His people.

Thus the invitation of Isaiah 1:18: " 'Come now, let us reason together,' says the LORD: 'Though your sins are like scarlet, they shall be as white as snow; though they are red like crimson, they shall become like wool.' "

Although now a harlot (v. 21) chasing after idols, Judah would be Yahweh's faithful bride once more (vv. 25–26). Now unrighteous and polluted, Judah would be purged, cleansed, and restored, not by working at it, jumping through more hoops, or whipping up God's pity by performing more religious rituals, but by simply coming to the one they had offended and admitting their need.

King Uzziah is dead. King Jotham is dead now too. Even the great Assyrian ruler Tiglath-Pileser has passed into the dust of time. But the Lord, the King who sits on an eternal throne high and lifted up still lives. He lives forever. He's alive and well for your sake. And His Son who was crowned with thorns and drenched with scarlet and crimson is seated at His right hand. And He will come again in glory—for you.

Lord, open our eyes so that we can see clearly just as Isaiah saw. We ask for Your mercy to remind us of Your great love for us even in our deepest need. Let us see on these pages the promises of forgiveness in Christ Jesus for us, for each of us personally, even in our ugliest sin.

Concluding Activities

Distribute the enrichment magazine and encourage participants to read it as part of their weekly study. Make any necessary announcements.

Close by singing or speaking together the words of the first stanza of "Today Your Mercy Calls Us" (*LW*, 347), or by speaking the words of the prayer found in the study leaflet. Follow this by reading 1 John 1:8–9 to the group.

The Day of the LORD

Isaiah 2–5

Preparing for the Session

Central Focus

In these chapters, Isaiah confronts God's people with their sins of pride and idolatry. He unmasks their smug self-satisfaction and describes the coming "day of the LORD," the day of God's judgment and wrath.

But God's prophet also preaches the Gospel, saying, "Come, let us go up to the mountain of the LORD . . . that He may teach us His ways and that we may walk in His paths" (Isaiah 2:3).

Objectives

That the participant, led by the Holy Spirit through the Word, will

1. see clearly the implications of God's wrath and judgment on human sin;
2. identify in Judah's sins of pride and idolatry his or her own rebellion and disobedience;
3. receive the grace and goodness of God in His forgiveness won for him or her by the "branch of the LORD," our Savior, Jesus; and
4. grow in a life of fruitfulness as he or she continues to "abide in the vine," drawing strength from Him.

Note for the small-group leaders: Lesson notes and other materials you will need begin on page 54.

For the Lecture Leader

Session Plan

Worship

Begin the session with the hymn and prayer printed in the study leaflet. Hymn accompaniments are available in denominational hymnals, such as *Lutheran Worship* (refer to hymnal index). (Note: Concordia Publishing House has available *Every Voice a Song,* a 9-CD set of organ accompaniments for 180 hymns and liturgy. All the initial worship hymns in the LifeLight courses are included in this resource. It's especially helpful for mission congregations and small parishes. See the list of study resources on page 7.)

Lecture Presentation

Introduction

Close your eyes. Go ahead. Close them. Now think about a time you felt at peace. Imagine the waves lapping against the rocks on the shore. Or the arm of a loved one around your shoulder as you walked together. Or the sound of the doctor's voice speaking the blessed word *benign.* Or the faint scents of wine and burning candle wax as you knelt at the altar and awaited the touch of your Lord in the Sacrament.

(Pause 10–15 seconds; give participants time to recall and relax in their memory.)

Peace. It's wonderful, isn't it? Perhaps we value it so much because we experience it so seldom. If human beings have proven anything, it's that we're incapable of bringing peace into our own hearts or relationships. And even when we do experience peace temporarily, we're never quite able to sustain it.

Optimists keep trying to bring us into a time of world peace. They arbitrate and mediate. They preach and propose utopias. They send ambassadors and sponsor conferences, all in an effort to produce peace.

The optimists cry, "Peace, peace." But there is no peace. There is so little outward peace because there is so little inward peace. The sinful human heart seethes with unrest, greed, and most critically, rebellion against God and His law.

Peace has never broken out in the world because peace—true peace with God—has so seldom broken through human hardness to make its home in human hearts. True peace is beyond human comprehension. That's why it must come to us as a gift, God's gift.

1 The Peace of the Lord (Isaiah 2:1–4)

Isaiah begins chapter 2 with a poem that describes the peace to come "in the latter days." When are these latter days? The Bible most often uses this phrase to refer to the coming Messiah and to the time that would follow His appearing. The Prince of Peace would come in the latter days, and He would bring His people peace. How would He accomplish that?

Verses 2–3—The poem itself pivots on a central, critical thought:

"He may teach us His ways . . . that we may walk in His paths."

We cannot walk in the paths of God's peace unless He teaches us.

But first He must draw us to Himself. The poem pictures people of all nations, a river of humanity, streaming up to the "mountain of the LORD." A river flowing uphill defies the laws of gravity. Then the mountain itself grows. Twenty-five-hundred-foot Zion surpasses twenty-nine-thousand-foot Everest to become a spiritual giant. Barring miracles, such things don't happen. Rivers don't run uphill, mountains don't climb, and sinful human beings do not spontaneously long for closeness with a holy God either. Barring a miracle, we avoid Him; we run from Him.

But a miracle has occurred. Jesus was lifted up on Golgotha. Mount Calvary became in a very real sense "the mountain of the LORD." Jesus promised that when He was lifted up, He would draw all people to Himself (John 12:32). And He did. At Pentecost, thousands fell on their knees to proclaim that Jesus Christ is Lord. They brought glory to the Father, and the Father poured out His peace into their hearts.

The miracle that happened that day is the miracle that keeps on happening and that will keep on happening as long as the earth stands. Our Lord keeps calling, gathering, inviting, and drawing sinners to Himself. He keeps on giving people His peace, one heart at a time.

The peace that fills our hearts changes our lives, and as we change, we also change the society around us. As the Scriptures declare, that change will not be complete here on earth. Even so, the peace Christ offers is no illusion. It's no empty promise. It's here. It's now. It's a precious gift to each of His subjects from the Prince of Peace Himself.

Verse 4—When our Lord Jesus does come again, His reign of peace will fully invade the hearts of the faithful. As His family, we will live in perfect peace with Him and with one another forever.

Until then, we rest in His promise, and we invite others to receive His peace (v. 3): "Come, let us go up to the mountain of the LORD, to the house of the God of Jacob."

2 The Pride of God's People (Isaiah 2:5–22)

The people of Isaiah's time wanted peace on earth—by human definition. They wanted a god they could manipulate. They sought economic security and relished their silver and gold (v. 7). They sought military security and relied on war horses and chariots (v. 7). They designed their own methods of issuing religious security and multiplied idols (v. 8) while they sought psychics (v. 6). They were secure—secure in their sins.

So Isaiah, burning with zeal for God and love for the people, delivered a stinging message of Law, a message designed to shake the complacency out of the people's hearts. Verses 12–22 describe the folly of human pride and the security blankets we humans try so desperately to weave together from the rags of our own accomplishments and abilities.

Every knee will bow. Every tongue will confess that Jesus Christ is Lord. We will bow in reverent love or in wide-eyed spasms of terror, but we will bow.

Verses 20–22—The Israelite carpenters and smiths created their pagan gods locally from carved wood or cast metal. A typical idol was covered with gold or silver and had its eye sockets plastered to make them white. The people would gather under trees to worship these idols and offer sacrifices, including the sacrificing of children. But in that day, the wicked would throw their idols over their shoulders in a mad dash for a cave in which to hide from the terror of the Lord as He poured out His wrath on the ungodly.

The phrase "in that day" is a favorite for Isaiah. He uses it fifty times. This major prophetic theme appears in 2:11. The expression can mean a particular time or some future event (e.g., the invasion of the Assyrians in the eighth century; 7:18, 20, 23), but it most often means Judgment Day.

3 The Judgment that Purifies (Isaiah 3:1–4:6)

How different for those in Christ. The Day of the Lord—the final day of judgment and Christ's second coming—will bring full peace for those who love Christ and full judgment for those who reject His gracious gift of salvation and eternal life. But we experience that peace even now, and we see that judgment fall even now.

The apostle Paul tells us, "God's kindness is meant to lead you to repentance" (Romans 2:4). Though we fall into sin, He continues to love and bless us. He coaxes, urges, and invites us to return to Him in repentance and faith. In love, He lets us experience the consequences of our actions. In love, He calls us to account.

That, in essence, is what was happening to the people in Judah. All would fall. Isaiah, the mighty seer, saw it. He warned the people. Still, most weren't ready to hear.

Verses 1–15 of chapter 3 describe a catastrophic leadership crisis:

• Verse 1—Supplies of food and water would disappear, setting up conditions of severe need among the people.

• Verses 2–3—Heroes, warriors, judges, prophets, counselors, craftsmen—anyone with any skill, experience, or ability in making decisions, giving orders, organizing others for specific tasks, giving advice, making laws, or protecting society—would all die or be deported.

• Verses 4, 12—The leadership vacuum created by war and political defeat would be filled by children who lack the ability, wisdom, and perspective to govern well.

• Verse 5—Anarchy would result. The rule of law would give way to the rule of the jungle. No one would respect any authority except the authority of brute force.

• Verse 6—No one would even want to lead. Note the "qualifications" for leaders given in this verse: "You have a cloak; you shall be our leader."

Despite the disaster that will befall them, the people will refuse to confess their sin. Brazen to the end, they will remain as impenitent as Sodom. They will continue to speak and act in rebellion against the Lord, and they will not even try to hide that fact (vv. 8–9).

The outcome would be clear. Those who were righteous (v. 10) would receive from the Lord's gracious hand rewards for the righteous deeds they had done. But those who were wicked would receive their just deserts.

What distinguished the righteous from the wicked? Then, as now, it was God's grace through faith.

All in Judah who believed in the Messiah, whom God had promised to send, received that righteousness. But those who refused God's gift, those who hardened their hearts and thought they had no need for God's righteousness, faced the storm of God's judgment alone. They had no place to hide, no place of shelter. Then as now, those who reject mercy receive justice. Isaiah 3:9 says it well: "Woe to their soul!" (NKJV)

Verses 13–15—The leaders in Judah were no better than the people. They bore special responsibility, not only for their own personal sin, but also for leading the nation astray. They had "devoured the [Lord's] vineyard." The very people who by virtue of their office as God's representatives should have set an example of righteousness and fruitful, godly living, had plundered the poor instead.

The Lord did not take this lightly. Nor did He take it impersonally. Note the "My people" of verse 15.

Verses 16–26—The unrighteousness of Judah's leaders did not excuse the people for their pride. Ignoring the poor, the women of Judah preened and primped themselves. But soon, all the perfume, scarves, nose rings and earrings, gowns and ankle bracelets, cosmetics and party dresses would disappear. Complete justice would overtake the proud and the selfish.

Isaiah 4:1—Many of Judah's men would die in battle or be deported. Judah's women would experience the shame and victimization known by women and children who had no men to support or defend them in that culture. How markedly different from the views of modern feminism! Seven women would beg every man who escaped death or capture, "Let us earn our own living. We won't burden you. But give us your name. Take away our social shame and the defenselessness of widowhood."

Isaiah's horrifying picture of judgment ends with a

picture of grace (4:2–6). We see the Lord once again stretching out arms of welcome toward His disobedient people. Isaiah 2:1–4 and 5:2–6 stand as bookends of grace, framing the threats of judgment that come in between. Both Law and Gospel have the heart of God as their source, the heart that cries out for the salvation of His people.

As at the beginning of chapter 2, the grace expressed at the end of chapter 4 offers peace to all who will receive it. Again, the Lord takes the initiative. He provides the blessings that make peace possible.

- Verse 3—He declares His people holy.
- Verse 4—He washes away the filth of their sins. He uses the fires of judgment to burn away the impurities of their hearts.
- Verses 5–6—Just as He provided for His people in the wilderness after they left Egypt, so He will continue to provide light in times of darkness, shade when His people find themselves taking heat, and a place of refuge and shelter from life's storms.

The branch who was to come would make that cleansing, purifying, sheltering work of God possible. Ancient Jewish sources such as the Aramaic Targums naturally associated the "branch" of 4:2 with the Messiah. But later commentators as far back as John Calvin (1509–64) have rejected this interpretation. They contend that while "branch" (v. 2a) could refer to the Messiah, its poetic parallel "fruit of the land" (v. 2b) certainly could not. Therefore, these interpreters conclude that the branch must talk about Israel, not the Messiah.

However, reflection on the care of a vineyard and on the variety in Hebrew poetry may offer a better explanation. After a grapevine is pruned back—an image of judgment in the Scriptures—one sees only the dry gray and black bark of the vine. Life appears absent. But with the change of seasons comes sudden new growth. Vivid green branches rapidly shoot out of the vine. Leaves unfold, and fruit clusters soon appear. In a matter of weeks, the dead-looking vines become beautiful and begin to produce fruit.

What an excellent picture of the coming of the Messiah and the blessings to follow His appearing! Instead of viewing the "branch" and "fruit of the land" as strict poetic parallels, one should see a progression in those verses as the promise of the Messiah and His blessings unfold. (See Psalm 1:1–3 for an example of progressive thought in Hebrew poetry.)

4 The Planting of the Lord (Isaiah 5:1–7)

The song of the vineyard starts out like a passage from Solomon's Song of Songs. The repetition of "beloved" and the faithful care he shows for cultivating the vineyard provide a romantic scene. Though we do not know the context in which the prophet first delivered this song, we can easily imagine contented guests lounging on cushions around a table as the song begins. The table is covered with plates of food but, more important, cups of wine. Conversation is polite. The atmosphere is relaxed. Swiftly the singer reaches the questions in verse 4. The guests have only a moment to ponder them. Then suddenly the song vigorously accuses and condemns the wine-sipping guests. Perhaps Isaiah never delivered his song in this surprising way, but even a singing or reading of this passage at the temple would have brought a shocked reaction from the people of Judah.

As the song crashes to this abrupt end, Isaiah explains its meaning in no uncertain terms. The people of Judah were the planting of the Lord. He had lovingly tended His vineyard. He had cared for them. He had guarded them. He had provided all they needed and had every right to expect fruitfulness—lives of increasing godliness—from them. Instead, when He went to gather His fruit, He found only oppression and injustice.

As New Testament believers though, we have an advantage because we've heard our Lord Jesus—the one who Himself is the branch of whom Isaiah wrote—explain this truth further. We've heard His words from John 15 (1–5):

> "I am the true vine, and My Father is the vinedresser. Every branch of Mine that does not bear fruit He takes away, and every branch that does bear fruit He prunes, that it may bear more fruit. Already you are clean because of the word that I have spoken to you. Abide in Me, and I in you. As the branch cannot bear fruit by itself, unless it abides in the vine, neither can you, unless you abide in Me. I am the vine; you are the branches. Whoever abides in Me

and I in him, he it is that bears much fruit, for apart from Me you can do nothing."

5 Woe to Those . . . (Isaiah 5:8–30)

Too often when we read the Old Testament, we come away with this attitude: "Boy, weren't those Israelites foolish? They couldn't see God's will for their lives at all. I'm sure glad we're not so foolish today." Such a response only demonstrates our flabby spirituality. The young lions of justice lick their lips in anticipation.

Exercise your faith by examining your life in view of Isaiah's woes in 5:8–22. See in these woes not simply a condemnation of sinful actions, but a call to righteous actions. Ask yourself these questions: Do I protect the property of others (v. 8)? Am I addicted to the deeds of the Lord (v. 11)? Do I promote righteousness in my community (v. 18)? Am I speaking up for the truth (v. 20)? Can I walk away from my mirror (v. 21)? Do I defend the innocent (vv. 22–23)?

Also recognize that for every woe spoken through the prophet Isaiah, your Savior has a word of blessing. He protects you as His very own child. He breaks your addiction to your favorite sins. He promotes you before the heavenly Father. He *is* the truth. He shatters the mirror of self-righteousness and in His wisdom declares you righteous by His suffering, death, and resurrection.

When Jesus hung on the cross at Calvary, His arms were outstretched so that the Father's arms could stretch out wide in love and welcome you and me. I'm so thankful I can fall into those arms of love and receive His forgiveness and peace, aren't you? Let's thank Him for that right now.

Concluding Activities

Ask the participants about their use of the enrichment magazine. Encourage participants to read it as part of their weekly study. Then distribute the study leaflet for the next session. Pray the following prayer:

O Lord, Your mercies are new to us every morning. Great is Your faithfulness! We run to Your arms and find rest there. We cherish Your gracious promises that as we simply abide in the vine, we will produce much fruit. Continually remind us that without You we can do nothing—not a few things, not the easy things, but nothing. Strip us of all self-righteousness, and continually assure us of the perfect righteousness that is ours in Christ Jesus. In His name we pray. Amen.

Oh, Come, Oh, Come, Immanuel!

Isaiah 7:1–9:7

Preparing for the Session

Central Focus

Isaiah wrote eloquently about the sign of Immanuel. This promise from God was for ancient Judah what it is for us today—a two-edged sword. Jesus is our Immanuel.

Objectives

That the participant, led by the Holy Spirit through the Word, will

1. understand the sign of Immanuel as both God's Word of Law and His Word of Gospel to His people;
2. repent for trying to take the responsibility for his or her salvation into his or her own hands;
3. give praise to Jesus, our Immanuel, for the complete deliverance He has earned for us.

Note for the small-group leaders: Lesson notes and other materials you will need begin on page 57.

For the Lecture Leader

Session Plan

Worship

Begin the session with the hymn and prayer printed in the study leaflet. Hymn accompaniments are available in denominational hymnals, such as *Lutheran Worship* (refer to hymnal index). (Note: Concordia Publishing House has available *Every Voice a Song*, a 9-CD set of organ accompaniments for 180 hymns and liturgy. All the initial worship hymns in the LifeLight courses are included in this resource. It's especially helpful for mission congregations and small parishes. See the list of study resources on page 7.)

Lecture Presentation

1 God's Word of Promise (Isaiah 7:1–9)

Oh, come, oh, come, Immanuel. Isaiah's great prophecy of Immanuel immediately makes us think of Christmas and of the Advent season of waiting and preparation. Indeed, the whole Old Testament is an Advent season of sorts as God's people waited for God to deliver them. This expectation gave them hope and courage to face the pressures and problems of day-to-day life.

They were the people of God, yet very often God seemed far away. There were dangers to peace and security all around: those who were opposed to God's people, enemies from without and inept leaders from within. There were the constant temptations of sin and selfishness, the temptations that we know so very well today just as God's people have always known them. All these things threatened to damage and even destroy God's holy people.

The ultimate issue was their salvation, eternal security, and relationship with God. The essential problem they faced was that they, like all of us, preferred to take matters into their own hands rather than simply kneel and humbly receive the grace and mercy of God.

As we consider the fulfillment of the great Immanuel prophecy from the texts we read for this lesson and as we consider what these texts mean for us in our world today, we remember that God gave this prophecy to real people who lived in a real world with real problems not at all unlike our own.

The story began back in chapter 6, the text we looked at in our first lesson. It was the year in which King Uzziah died. God's people faced an uncertain future. But then Isaiah received God's commission. He would speak to a people who "have ears to hear, but hear not" and "have eyes to see, but see not" (Ezekiel 12:2). And so we arrive at chapter 7, Exhibit A of just such a person—the king, the human king of Judah, King Ahaz!

2 The Strong Assyrian Army

The people of God stare into the face of a seemingly overwhelming threat. The rise of the Assyrian Empire has upset the delicate balance of power in the Middle East. Assyria is poised to take control. The Assyrians appear ready to rise and conquer. Judah's neighbors to the north, Israel and Syria, have formed a defensive alliance in the hope—the vain hope, as it turned out—of resisting Assyrian aggression.

Eager to amass as much defensive power as possible, Israel (Northern Kingdom) and Syria invite Ahab of Judah (Southern Kingdom) to join their coalition. When he refuses, they invade Judah in an attempt to depose Ahaz and place their own puppet, the son of Tabeel, on the throne of David.

As this chapter begins, Ahaz inspects Jerusalem's aqueduct, preparing for a siege (7:1–3). Ahaz ponders three choices:

1. Capitulate to the allied forces.

2. Make his own alliance with Assyria against Syria.

3. Try to go it alone.

Yahweh sends His spokesman Isaiah to Ahaz with a fourth option, a striking alternative: Trust God! The Lord would deliver His people. He would save them. In fact, only His hands could work salvation for them.

But Ahaz thought he knew better. He thought it safer to take the responsibility for his own security and for that of his people. He wanted to hold his own fate in his own hands. From 2 Kings 16:7 on, we learn that Ahaz rejected God's option. He chose the second option instead—he entered into an alliance with Assyria. He paid a hefty tribute to Tiglath-Pileser—the price of impenitence.

Rebellion. Unbelief. Arrogance. Ahaz racked up sin upon sin. But in addition to all these affronts to God's holiness in forming this alliance, Ahaz also compromised his witness.

3 The Price of Impenitence

Has anything like this ever happened in your life? What kind of prices have you paid to avoid repentance?

When you sin, and you know it, do you ever harbor guilt for that sin for hours and days rather than instantly going to your heavenly Father for forgiveness and cleansing? Have you ever told yourself that you were not sorry enough to confess your sin? If so, you are trying in a small way to save yourself, to somehow earn God's compassion, to make up for your disobedience, and to repair the breach yourself.

Whenever we refuse to admit our helplessness, our utter and total need for our Savior, we pay a price for our independence. We pay the price of impenitence. We also compromise our witness. We rob ourselves of the abundant life our Lord died to earn for us. Jesus hung on the cross so we wouldn't have to bear our guilt alone. Jesus died so we could say, "I'm sorry" to God and to one another in true, God-given humility. We need not save ourselves. We need not trust ourselves. We dare not—we must not—try.

4 God's Promised Presence (Isaiah 7:10–25)

Despite Ahaz's reluctance to trust God's Word of promise, Isaiah announced a sign anyway, an earthly sign to which God would bind His promised presence. A child would be born whose very name, *Immanuel*, means "God with us." A sign signaled salvation (v. 16): "before the boy knows how to refuse the evil and choose the good, the land whose two kings you dread will be deserted." The threat of the northern coalition would be over. Ahaz and Judah, king and people, would be spared.

Note that Isaiah reports a similar sign a little later (8:3). Isaiah's wife conceived their second son, who also bore a symbolic name: Maher-shalal-hashbaz (swift the booty; speedy the prey). The boy's name indicated a swift conclusion to the threat of war. The northern coalition would quickly become the prey and booty of Assyria (8:4).

But the Assyrian army would not stop at Judah's border. Look carefully at Isaiah's words in 8:6–8. Ahaz and his people refused the peaceful waters of Shiloah, a stream within the walls of Jerusalem that symbolized God's presence in the lives of His people. Ahaz had instead chosen waters that seemed more powerful—those of the great Euphrates River that ran through Assyria. Those waters, however, would become a tsunami for Ahaz and his people. Assyria would sweep over Judah to fill the whole land of Immanuel (8:8). In his attempt to retain control, Ahaz had lost it completely.

And so the sign of Immanuel, "God with us," had a bad side too. Isaiah, the mighty seer, saw terrible days ahead. These days would be worse than any that God's people had seen since Israel itself was divided, since the days the Northern Kingdom seceded from the Southern Kingdom, and the people of God lost their unity of life and purpose. The North would fall to Assyria, and so eventually would Judah. God's people would be plundered. Assyria would leave Judah barren and bare (7:20), shaved of all its crops and cattle.

5 God's Plan of Salvation (Isaiah 8:1–10)

Immanuel. God with us. It's a two-edged sword.

Isaiah had experienced the danger of God's presence in a personal way as he stood in the presence of the holy God and recognized his sinfulness. Now Ahaz would realize this same truth, but he would not turn to God in humble confession of sin as Isaiah had. He would turn up his nose at God's grace and receive instead God's justice.

We cannot take grace for granted. Rejecting the Lord's power and promise to save leads always and only to spiritual disaster. The sign of Immanuel stands as a warning to us all—to all the peoples of all the earth. The best-laid plans of mere mortals will not deliver or truly save.

You know the saying: "Man proposes; God disposes." Isaiah spoke the same thought (8:10): "Take counsel together, but it will come to nothing; speak a word, but it will not stand, for God is with us."

Still, the meaning of Immanuel is also a message of comfort, precisely because there is no other source of salvation. God's promised presence is a sign to us that there is hope. He is with us! Whatever our plans or whatever plans others may devise for us or against us, none of those plans will stand. When we seem to lose control, when our lives and the world in which we live seem totally out of control, even then—especially then—God is with us.

When it comes to the very essentials of life, and the questions of eternal life and eternal death, not only is God with us, but God has also come as one of us.

"The virgin shall conceive and bear a son, and they shall call His name Immanuel," St. Matthew the evangelist writes in Matthew 1:23. Here the Holy Spirit reveals the fulfillment of Isaiah's prophetic Word. God is with us in the flesh, because the "Word became flesh and dwelt among us" (John 1:14). We see both edges of the sword flash in the light of the Son, Jesus Christ, our Immanuel. We see God's justice in punishing human sin and His mercy in punishing—not us—but His own dear Son, our substitute.

In the incarnation of Christ, God's presence has come to earth. As we wait for His visible return to judge the living and the dead, God has bound His promised presence among us to earthly signs: to water; to bread and wine; to the word of forgiveness, of absolution, spoken from the forgiving lips of our pastor. As surely as we can see, touch, taste, and hear these signs, we know God is with us.

As for Judah of old, God's presence with us can mean judgment:

For those who come to God humbly confessing their sins and need for grace, the sign of Immanuel brings God's salvation. Our Lord has taken us into His arms. He places into our hands, mouths, and hearts the very presence of Christ. On God's Word of promise, we stand confirmed in our faith in the salvation He has worked for us.

6 God's Promised Purpose (Isaiah 8:11–22)

Isaiah and Judah's believing remnant would continue to face an uncertain future. Many in Judah beside King Ahaz would demonstrate the truth of God's verdict: They had "ears to hear, but hear not," and "eyes to see, but see not" (Ezekiel 12:2). They would continue to reject the sign of God's promise and would turn instead to worldly sources of hope, false hope. Some would even turn (Isaiah 8:19–22) to the mediums, wizards, astrologers, and soothsayers that God had so often condemned as abominations.

Seeing only the darkness of despair around them, these impenitent sinners would refuse to believe that God could bring them light. Isaiah, the mighty seer, had seen that light. In the midst of darkness, he had seen the dawn. He continued to call his people to hope in the God who alone would bring that light into the gloom of a sinful world (9:2). Though Isaiah's message would be unacceptable to many as a stumbling block, a snare, and a trap (8:14), by grace a few would walk in that light, in the peaceful confidence of knowing the promise of Immanuel.

7 God's Prince of Peace (Isaiah 9:1–7)

After the darkness came dawn. Isaiah saw a future glorious in its brilliance. That day would not come to Jerusalem first, but to Galilee and the surrounding northern territory. This area would be the first to fall to the invading Assyrian armies. But the first to groan in gloom would be the first to glow in glory. "The people who walked in darkness have seen a great light," Isaiah shouts in 9:2.

Again, St. Matthew points out how God kept His Word of promise in Jesus who began His ministry in Galilee of the Gentiles (Matthew 4:12–17). From such backwater, from such an unassuming starting point, Jesus would make His way to Jerusalem. He would enter the capital as the Son of David. He would establish the throne of His ancestor David forever. Like His humble birth in the town of David, Jesus' accession to the throne would not happen in the way of a human king. Riding on a donkey, He would come not to be served, but to serve and to give His life as a ransom for many. Through His humble and holy sacrifice on the cross, He would absorb the wrath of God for all our sins—yours, mine, the sins of all the world.

The whole New Testament age is an Advent season of sorts. God's people wait for their Lord to come again. That expectation gives us hope and courage to face the pressures and problems of day-to-day life.

God has bound His Word of promise and presence to a sign. God is with us. He is Immanuel, David's Son and David's Lord. In His very body and blood, He assures us of His presence and touches us with His forgiveness. He gave that body and shed that blood for the forgiveness of all our sins. He is with us, and He will be with us until Immanuel comes again.

Concluding Activities

Encourage comments or questions about the content of the enrichment magazine. Make any necessary announcements. Then distribute the study leaflet for the next session.

Close by singing or speaking together the words of "Oh, Come, Oh, Come, Emmanuel" from the study leaflet.

His Hand Is Stretched Out Still

Isaiah 9:8–12:6

Preparing for the Session

Central Focus

God's hand is stretched out in judgment on all who rebel against Him. God's hand of judgment fell fully on Christ Jesus, the Prince of Peace, great David's greater Son, who hung on the cross and absorbed all of God's wrath against human sin. As we look forward to the coming of that Kingdom in all its fullness, we continue to spread the Good News of that Kingdom so that our God's great name may be known on all the earth.

Objectives

That the participant, led by the Holy Spirit through the Word, will

1. better understand God's justice and mercy, especially as the two can be described in the words "His hand is stretched out still";
2. see himself or herself as among the remnant, the believing saints whom God has delivered from judgment and restored as citizens of the Messiah's peaceful kingdom; and
3. trust more deeply in the God who is our strength, song, and salvation.

Note for the small-group leaders: Lesson notes and other materials you will need begin on page 60.

For the Lecture Leader

Session Plan

Worship

Begin the session with the hymn and prayer printed in the study leaflet. Hymn accompaniments are available in denominational hymnals, such as *Lutheran Worship* (refer to hymnal index). (Note: Concordia Publishing House has available *Every Voice a Song,* a 9-CD set of organ accompaniments for 180 hymns and liturgy. All the initial worship hymns in the LifeLight courses are included in this resource. It's especially helpful for mission congregations and small parishes. See the list of study resources on page 7.)

Lecture Presentation

Introduction

Classic movie fans recognize the line "A fine mess you've gotten us into, Ollie!" Most often when Laurel used this line, he and Hardy could each take equal credit for the fine mess.

In the Bible reading for this past week, God's people had gotten themselves into a fine mess too, and there was nothing comical about either that mess or about the blame shifting and excuse making in which they were engaged.

Israel and Syria camped on Jerusalem's doorstep in an attempt to force Judah to join forces with them to resist the Assyrian onslaught that was sure to come. Something had to be done! Everyone in the kingdom knew it.

Still, Isaiah saw more than doom and destruction. He saw the grace and mercy of God, who would not abandon His people forever. God was not finished with Judah just yet. Even though the tree of David would be hacked down, a new branch—a righteous branch—would sprout up. The God of wrath was also the God of mercy who would make forgiveness and new life possible.

1 Woe to Israel and Judah (Isaiah 9:8–10:4)

What a mess God's people had gotten themselves into! First, they had split David's kingdom in two parts, north and south, Israel and Judah. During the centuries that followed, they quarreled with and attacked each other, each claiming to be the true heir of God's promise.

Lest we think, "How could they?" we need to recall that modern nations have split into north and south. Churches have split into east and west. Battles often erupt in the Church still today. And if not open warfare, we have the kind of guerrilla action that subtly slices through relationships, damaging and even destroying our joy, unity, witness, and even sometimes the souls of our brothers and sisters.

So North stood toe-to-toe with South. Factions even developed within the Northern Kingdom between the two largest tribes, Manasseh and Ephraim. One might conclude that only their animosity for their cousins in the Southern Kingdom united them.

Through Isaiah, God spoke loud and clear about these factions. The lives and futures of all God's people were interlocked and connected. God claims us individually as His own, to be sure. But He has also made us His people—in one body. The people of Israel had lost sight of this. They had forgotten that their God had called and gathered them around His very presence in His holy temple.

But the problem lay deeper still. Through Isaiah, the Holy Spirit touches the precise spot from which all the infection in Israel's heart has grown. God's people have turned against each other because they have turned against their God. They have chosen to trust themselves, as well as their own plans and purposes for their own lives.

Remember Maher-shalal-hashbaz? Remember that Isaiah chose a name for his son that meant "quick to the booty, speedy to the prey"? No enemy soldiers needed to attack. The leaders of Israel themselves robbed the poor and needy of the land. In 10:2, widows became their spoil and orphans their plunder. "Woe to you all," Isaiah shouted in the open square.

But very few listened. Fewer still cared. The people refused to believe that their difficulties were only the appetizer. They refused to accept the idea that God was about to dish up a seven-course serving of His wrath. No one would escape.

The people to whom Isaiah spoke thought they could withstand any storm. In fact, they believed that things in their lives were about to get bigger and better.

Verses 9–10—Bricks have fallen. We will rebuild with smooth stones! The fig trees have been cut down. We will rebuild with cedars!

In today's language, their chorus might go: "We lost the first house, but we'll rebuild. We'll build something bigger, better, more luxurious, and certainly more secure. The new house won't fall. Not ever. We'll see to it!"

But God's hand was stretched out still. His anger was not turned away. God was not finished with them, not at all. The house would fall again. It would collapse into a pile of rubble never—in the Northern Kingdom—to be rebuilt.

Even while God stretched out His arm in judgment over the people of the Northern Kingdom (Israel), the people of Judah continued their own stroll down the path of independence. You will remember that Judah's King Ahaz planned to appeal for help. He directed His appeal—not to the Lord who made heaven and earth—but to the empire of Assyria that was making a name for itself among the powers of that day.

Assyria, the very foe that had thrown Syria and Israel in bed together in defensive alliance, was now—if Ahaz got his way—to become Judah's friend! The gulf between the two factions in God's family would become wider than ever before.

2 Woe to Assyria (Isaiah 10:5–19)

According to commentator John N. Oswalt, Isaiah's teaching in 10:5–19 was revolutionary. Typically, religions of this time taught that war between nations was also a war between the gods of those nations. The people who won had the strongest gods. However, Isaiah teaches that the almighty Yahweh will give the Assyrians victory over His own people!

Verse 13—The God who raises up nations and establishes kingdoms slipped His hand inside the Assyrian glove. Some in Judah may have understood this, but certainly not Assyria's king. He took credit for his victory. God heard his words: "By the strength of my hand I have done it, and by my wisdom." Whose hand?

Verse 14—God answered such arrogance. He stretched His hand out against Assyria. Assyria's assignment against Judah had come to an end. It was finished. But God was not finished with Assyria's king. Not yet.

Verse 15—How easily we forget. How easily we creatures imagine ourselves to be the Creator. How easily the pot forgets it's clay formed by a potter. How easily the tool forgets it's iron, forged by a blacksmith for his own purposes. Look at my successes! See what my hands have accomplished! Whose hands?

Verse 16—God stretched out His hand against Assyria, just as His hand is always outstretched against any and all who exalt themselves and rebel against their deliverer. In Isaiah's time, no greater army marched on the face of the earth. But the Assyrian Empire would fall. God would lay His ax at its base and reduce it to kindling.

Verse 17—Then He would set the kindling ablaze and turn it to ashes.

Sooner or later every earthly kingdom, every earthly ruler and all those ruled by them, will stand before God's upraised hand. Sooner or later all the rulers and all those ruled by them will stand at the judgment seat of Christ. They will stand before the One whose anger is not turned away, the God who is not finished with us. Not yet.

3 A Remnant Will Return (Isaiah 10:20–34)

Along with the prophet Jeremiah, Isaiah places great emphasis on God's promise to preserve a remnant of His people after their judgment and exile. Whereas earlier references to the remnant in 1:9 and 6:13 emphasize God's judgment that only a remnant will remain, the many references to the remnant in chapters 10 and 11 become a note of mercy and grace.

Verse 21—Isaiah speaks that merciful word as he assures the people of the remnant that would return. Remember that Isaiah had given his firstborn son a name that meant "a remnant shall return" (7:3).

That name carries God's double meaning. It speaks of God's punishment: Judah would be conquered, her people led off into exile, and only a remnant would remain. Nevertheless, a remnant *would* remain. In mercy, God would preserve a handful of His people.

Verses 24–25—"Be not afraid of the Assyrians," the Lord called out to His people through Isaiah. "For in a very little while My fury will come to an end, and My anger will be directed to their destruction." The yoke (v. 27) they've laid on your shoulders will be broken. Egypt (v. 24) oppressed you centuries ago, and look what happened to them at the Red Sea. Midian (v. 26) oppressed you long ago, and the Lord slaughtered them at the rock of Oreb (see Judges 7:25). So don't be afraid. Those who repent can rely on the God who saves, the God who has promised His continuing presence among His people, the God who gave the sign of Immanuel.

Following the vision about the remnant of God's people, Isaiah immediately records another vision about the threatening approach of the Assyrian army in 10:28–34. Through short, punchy sentences, the prophet traces the army's progress from about fifteen miles north of Jerusalem along the edge of the Jordan Rift Valley, bypassing the city's outer defensive towns: Gibeon, Ramah, and Gibeah.

4 God Isn't Finished Yet (Isaiah 11:1–16)

Down though the centuries, artists have tried to capture the essence of the Lord's peaceable kingdom on canvas. Isaiah first painted this picture, not in visual images, but in words. Listen to some of them (11:6–9):

> The wolf shall dwell with the lamb, the leopard shall lie down with the young goat, and the calf and the lion and the fattened calf together; and a little child shall lead them. The cow and the bear shall graze, their young shall lie down together, and the lion shall eat straw like the ox. The nursing child shall play near the hole of the cobra, and the weaned child shall put his hand on the adder's den. They shall not hurt or destroy in all My holy mountain; for the earth shall be full of the knowledge of the LORD as the waters cover the sea.

This is quite a sharp contrast to the thunder of armies marching back and forth across the Mideast, and quite a contrast to the councils of war and the fear-filled hearts of so many in Isaiah's day—and in ours.

Quite likely Isaiah's hearers asked, as we ask today, "How? How will this peace come about? Who could put together the kind of coalition that could make peace possible? When? And where?"

Good questions. Let's start with the question of who. Who could make such a thing possible? The line of David would be lopped off. The stump would look dead. But God wasn't finished. A shoot would grow from the stump—a new David, a second David, a better David.

This King would rule in perfect righteousness. This King would rule in the very Spirit of God. He would rule in the Spirit's wisdom, understanding, and strength. He would know and understand God perfectly, completely. He would bring a peace that passes our ability to comprehend it—the peace with which the Creator first established His creation before His creatures ruined it by their rebellion.

This new David would rule over all. He would rule over Judah and Israel, to be sure, but also over the Gentiles. God would gather His people—the remnant, those who survived His judgment—beneath this King's banner, beneath the cross. And even as He gathered them, He would send them forth under that banner into the whole world in the name of their new King.

(Mark 1:15) "The kingdom of God is at hand," John the Baptist announced.

(Matthew 6:10) "Your kingdom come!" Jesus taught His disciples to pray.

(Luke 23:42) "Jesus, remember me when You come into Your kingdom!" the dying thief prayed from his cross.

(Matthew 21:9) "Hosanna to the Son of David! Blessed is He who comes in the name of the Lord! Hosanna in the highest!" the children shouted on Palm Sunday.

And so we sing today as we worship, as we bow in reverence and prepare to receive the One who comes to us in His body and blood.

Isaiah spoke of this day, a day yet to come, when God would intervene in justice and righteousness, when God would gather His people from all nations to His holy mountain, when the jealous rivalry between Ephraim and Judah would cease, when all Israel—all the saints who have been called by Christ's name—would go forth like a mighty army to carry the banner of God's salvation to the ends of the earth.

But first comes God's judgment. It came on the Friday we now call "good," the day when God poured out His justice on the son of David, He who grew from the root—the stump—of Jesse. God poured out His wrath on the One who came to earth bearing the name Immanuel—God with us.

God wasn't finished on Good Friday. Not quite. Risen from the dead, Christ now sits at the right hand of the Father to intercede for us. Christ now sits at the right hand of the Father to rule and judge the world for the good of His Kingdom. Christ now sits at the right hand of the Father to bring to the hearts of His people the peace that passes all human understanding, the peace of a world forgiven and cleansed.

5 God's Hand of Anger Turned Away (Isaiah 12)

What a day! No wonder Isaiah bursts into a song of praise as he thinks of it. No wonder the Holy Spirit saw fit to record this hymn at this point in Isaiah's Book.

We join in those praises too. We, too, descend from that remnant. We have seen our punishment fall on Christ. We have seen Him take the wrath we ourselves so richly deserve. We, too, have laid our sins on Jesus, that spotless Lamb of God, great David's greater Son.

With those who walked in triumph through the Red Sea, with the hopeful remnant of Isaiah's day, with the saints of God gathered around His throne in heaven, we, too, sing the song of Moses and of the Lamb: (Exodus 15:2) "The LORD is my strength and my song, and He has become my salvation"; (Isaiah 12:5) "Sing praises to the Lord, for He has done gloriously; let this be made known in all the earth"; (Revelation 15:4) "Who will not fear, O Lord, and glorify Your name? For You alone are holy. All nations will come and worship You"; and (Isaiah 12:6) "Great in Your midst is the Holy One of Israel".

Those are all stanzas of the same song, all praising the same God—the God whose anger has been turned away in Christ. God was finally finished with us when our Savior cried out, "It is finished" (John 19:30). God's anger turned on Jesus and was turned away from us.

We continue to lift our praises to Him. Great in our midst, great in our lives, great in our worship, is the Holy One of Israel. Immanuel. God with us.

Concluding Activities

After any needed announcements, distribute the study leaflet for the next session. Close by praying the Lord's Prayer. Ask that participants speak more slowly than usual and that they pay particular attention to the petition "Your kingdom come" (Matthew 6:10).

Fallen Is Babylon the Great

Isaiah 13–17

Preparing for the Session

Central Focus

These chapters begin what Bible scholars have called the Gentile oracles. In the texts for this week, God condemns the Gentile nations for their rebellion and stubborn pride. Even as our Lord does that, He comforts His people with the promise that their oppression under these nations will soon come to an end.

But the Lord also has another purpose in mind for these acrid declarations of His judgment. As He confronts the nations with their sin, He also desires to lead them to repentance and faith in the Savior who is to come.

Objectives

That the participant, led by the Holy Spirit through the Word, will

1. understand Babylon as the world system that throughout history has set itself against God and against His Christ;
2. take comfort in the ultimate defeat of this world system;
3. recognize that by God's act of claiming us in Baptism, we are a people distinct and different from the nations;
4. use the Holy Spirit's power to resist the influences of the world, the devil, and his or her own flesh.

Note for the small-group leaders: Lesson notes and other materials you will need begin on page 63.

For the Lecture Leader

Session Plan

Worship

Begin the session with the hymn and prayer printed in the study leaflet. Hymn accompaniments are available in denominational hymnals, such as *Lutheran Worship* (refer to hymnal index). (Note: Concordia Publishing House has available *Every Voice a Song,* a 9-CD set of organ accompaniments for 180 hymns and liturgy. All the initial worship hymns in the LifeLight courses are included in this resource. It's especially helpful for mission congregations and small parishes. See the list of study resources on page 7.)

Lecture Presentation

Introduction

The chapters from Isaiah you read during the past week form the first half of what Bible scholars have called the Gentile oracles. They come as a kind of intermission.

Have you ever had to deliver bad news to someone? It's a tough business. The word used to describe Isaiah's visions against the nations is *massa.* Perhaps this word means "oracle," as usually appears in the translations, but it comes from a Hebrew word meaning "to lift up or carry." It may mean that the prophet lifted or carried his voice when speaking the oracle, or it may refer to the burden he placed on each nation he named.

Chapters 13–23 tell of God's judgment on specific nations around the Mideast at the time of Isaiah. In the first of these Gentile oracles, God condemns Babylon, Assyria, Philistia, Moab, Damascus, and Syria for their rebellion and stubborn pride. These chapters have two main purposes for then and now: calling for repentance from those who don't know the true God and comforting those who do know Him.

As our Lord has said so consistently throughout the Holy Scriptures, He desires all "to be saved and to come to the knowledge of the truth" (1 Timothy 2:4). Why? Because He loves all the people of all the nations; He wants to bring them into His family.

Our Lord also comforts His people with the promise that their oppression under the heel of the insolent and the unbelieving world will not last forever. He will bring His people relief.

As we study the message of these Gentile Oracles today, we will focus mostly on the great comfort Isaiah's words bring us as God's people. We will reaffirm the truth that the powers of the world system around us (Babylon), those powers that continually plague and persecute us, will eventually fall.

1 Babylon the Great (Genesis 11:1–9; Revelation 18:2–3)

Do you have a pet conspiracy theory? Such theories abound. The reading, viewing public never seems to tire of them.

For example, there's the aliens-have-landed-and-the-Air-Force-is-covering-it-up theory touted by the supermarket tabloids year after year.

More serious for their potential harm are the various theories that accuse specific racial or ethnic groups of conspiring to take over the world's economy or to overthrow one government or the other. Those in political power in Nazi Germany used just such a conspiracy theory to justify atrocities committed against the Jews.

Regardless of your opinion about who shot John Kennedy or about whether or not aliens from outer space have landed in the Mohave Desert, there's one conspiracy theory we as God's people cannot laugh off. We must regard this conspiracy with dead seriousness. Its code name? Babylon. Its purpose? Nothing less than the overthrow of God's rule and the renunciation of our Lord Christ.

(Genesis 11:1–9) "Let us make a name for ourselves," these rebels on the plain of Shinar decided. They set about to build a tower that would ensure them a place of prestige in history. They built their tower as a monument to their own great wisdom and amazing creativity.

This tower was more. It stood as a visible declaration of independence—independence from God. The creatures sought to honor themselves rather than their Creator.

You know the rest of the story. You know that our Lord had the final word. The tower of Babel stood unfinished on the plain of Shinar as a monument not to human creativity and wisdom but rather to the foolish rebellion of a sinful race.

Centuries later, the plain of Shinar would again become a seat of power, lying at the very center of the Babylonian Empire. In her glory days, this Babylon would subjugate most of the nations of the Mideast. The Babylonians would rout even the mighty Assyrian army.

But at the time of Isaiah, Babylon had not yet ascended to that kind of glory. Assyria, not Babylon, stood at the pinnacle of worldly power in Isaiah's day.

So why, if God wanted to comfort His people with the truth that one day He would rout their enemies, would Isaiah begin his denunciation of pagan powers with Babylon? Why not begin by lobbing verbal grenades at Assyria?

While no one knows for sure why Isaiah blasted away at Babylon first, we might propose one theory, a conspiracy theory, if you will.

As most Sunday School children know, human rebellion against God began in Eden when Adam and Eve disobeyed. But at Babel the human race organized its rebellion for what seems to have been the first time. For the first time, human beings (perhaps most of the human race living at the time) stood together and said no to God.

By the time the apostle John wrote the New Testament Book of Revelation, Babylon had become a symbol for any nation—in John's day it was Rome—that represented the pride of human power and ungodly independence.

As we read John's words, we cannot help but shudder as we see in our mind's eye the fire and smoke of destruction and as we hear the wailing cry of the peoples of the world, those who have sworn allegiance to the world's values, wisdom, and ways (Revelation 18:2–3 NKJV).

> Babylon the great is fallen, is fallen, and has become a dwelling place of demons, a prison for every foul spirit, and a cage for every unclean and hated bird! For all the nations have drunk of the

> wine of the wrath of her fornication . . . and the merchants of the earth have become rich through the abundance of her luxury.

2 Babylon—God's Tool (Isaiah 13:1)

Our fight will not last forever. The world system that turns up its nose at our God and at His Christ will someday acknowledge His lordship. Babylon will come crashing down. Our tormentors will drink the wine of our great King's wrath to the dregs.

Just as the Lord wants to comfort His people today with these truths, so He wanted to comfort those to whom Isaiah originally ministered. True enough, God would use ancient Babylonia just as He had used Assyria. That nation would serve His purposes. It would act as His tool, never even knowing the part it played in God's scheme of things.

God would use the armies of Babylon to bring the people of Judah to their knees in repentance. Unlike the citizens of the Northern Kingdom (Israel) who stiffened their necks in pride and resisted God's discipline, a remnant—a small group—of those from Judah who went into captivity would return home, chastened. The horrors of conquest and exile, strong medicine though it admittedly was, would bring about a cure. It would convince God's people once and for all of the folly of following false gods, bowing down to idols of gold and silver, and relying on themselves for help and hope.

Remember the strong denunciation of Assyria we read last time (Isaiah 10:12–19)? That nation convinced itself that it had conquered Israel by its own stealth and cunning, and in its own power. Today's readings tell us that Babylon would eventually fall into that same trap of pride (Isaiah 14:4–21).

Congratulating itself on the strength of its army, the strategies of its commanders, and the superiority of its culture, Babylon would feel the trap snap shut as God turned His anger from Judah and began to direct His wrath toward Judah's enemies (Isaiah 14:22–23).

3 The Wrath of God (Isaiah 13:1–13; Romans 1:18–32)

Let's look for a moment at the specifics of God's wrath as it has been and as it will be spent on Babylon—the wicked world system—throughout human history.

As chapter 13 begins, the Lord is about to pour out His wrath. He's rallying His armies (vv. 1–5) as He prepares to destroy His enemies. On that day, (Isaiah 13:6–9) the "day of the LORD . . . all hands will be feeble, and every human heart will melt. They will be dismayed: pangs and agony will seize them . . . They will look aghast at one another; their faces will be aflame. Behold, the day of the LORD comes."

On that day (v. 11), the Lord will "punish the world for its evil, and the wicked for their iniquity. [He] will put an end to the pomp of the arrogant and lay low the pompous pride of the ruthless." He will cut the proud off at the knees and call a halt to the arrogance of all tyrants.

"Yes!" we exclaim. "Go, God!" we shout. And we wonder when we'll see it. Maybe in the secret places of our hearts, deep down where we sometimes harbor the infection of discouragement, we wonder at times if we'll ever see it at all.

When we do that, we're forgetting Paul's words in Romans 1:18:

> The wrath of God is revealed from heaven against all ungodliness and unrighteousness of men, who by their unrighteousness suppress the truth.

Even now, the wrath of God is being revealed. You see, God's wrath doesn't always involve brimstone falling from heaven. We need not smell sulfur before we can let ourselves believe that God's wrath has come against the ungodly. Very often God's wrath falls in people's lives as He lets them have precisely what they say they want most!

Sometimes God reveals His wrath by letting those who rebel against Him hike down the path they have chosen for themselves until they reach its end. He knows that all the paths rebels choose for themselves—all of those paths—end up at the same dead end. Literally.

Those paths ultimately end in physical death, but they also end in spiritual death, eternal death. Death lies just down the road for all those who follow the maps of reality they buy at rest stops in Babylon.

Maybe you've heard of a mom or dad who caught a son or daughter smoking. Perhaps instead of taking the cigarettes away, that parent has forced the son or daughter to smoke every cigarette in the pack, one after the other. Perhaps these parents said, "So you want to smoke? Great! Smoke! Smoke all you want. Smoke to the full! Enjoy yourself!"

While this approach in disciplining may not be the best for every situation, it does, in a sense, picture God's wrath quite accurately. When those who reject God's rule rebel and rebel and rebel and insist on their own way and rebel and rebel . . . and rebel, finally, Scripture says (Romans 1:28), God will give them up to the very gods they have chosen for themselves.

Our heavenly Father always does this with a heavy heart, with a heart that cries out, "Why will you die?" (Ezekiel 33:11). Nevertheless, He does do it. He will not force anyone to love Him. He will not force anyone to obey Him.

God's wrath is being poured out right now, just as Paul says, in the lives of many people and into the world system human beings have insisted on constructing for themselves.

What are the results of God's wrath? Look back at Isaiah 13:7–8. God splashes this canvas with the somber colors of fear and grief, pain and disease. Isn't that exactly how you would characterize the lives of those around you who have committed themselves to the values of the world system? And even if you don't see evidence of God's wrath at just this moment, you can be sure—on the authority of God's Word—that it has already begun to fall.

4 The Prophet's Burdens (Isaiah 13:13–17:14)

No one will escape the wrath of God. No one is escaping even now. But one day, that wrath will roar down on the Babylon around us in an unprecedented way.

Listen to the description of that wrath. As you do so, think of it both in relationship to Old Testament Babylonia and to the Babylon we believers continue to battle today.

(As you get to this part of the lecture, read Isaiah 13:13–22 aloud to the group.)

Wow! What a picture! Isaiah piles detail upon detail as he describes the judgment that will fall on each of the nations he addressed in the Gentile oracles.

The details change from prophecy to prophecy, but the destruction and devastation remain the same. The citizens of those ancient nations have already, in spirit at least, joined in the funeral dirge St. John recorded centuries later (Revelation 18:2):

> Fallen, fallen is Babylon the great!

While those committed to the world system mourn, God's people heave a deep sigh of relief. Wickedness, powerful as it seems, will come to an end. Satan, powerful as he seems, will lose all his power to harass us. The yawning gates of death, ravenous though they may be, will someday close forever. Isaiah 14:12 says, "How you are fallen from heaven, O Day Star [Satan]," and in verse 15, "You are brought down to Sheol, to the far reaches of the pit."

We will stand safe and sound with our Savior. Babylon will fall. But don't give up, saints! Don't believe Satan's lie that God's kingdom is in retreat! Don't fall for the temptations of discouragement or despair! Our Lord, the Lord of grace and of glory, has the final word (Revelation 17:14):

> [Babylon] will make war against the Lamb, and the Lamb will conquer them, for He is Lord of lords and King of kings, and those with Him are called and chosen and faithful.

Amen. It shall be so. Praise the Lord, our God!

Concluding Activities

Distribute the study leaflet for the next session. Close with the benediction with which St. Paul blessed the believers at Thessalonica:

> Now may the God of peace Himself sanctify you completely, and may your whole spirit and soul and body be kept blameless at the coming of our Lord Jesus Christ. He who calls you is faithful; He will surely do it. (1 Thessalonians 5:23–24)

Hope for the Hopeless

Isaiah 18–23

Preparing for the Session

Central Focus

These chapters continue the Gentile oracles. They pronounce God's judgment against still more nations that have rebelled against God and insisted on going their own way. But besides hearing harsh words of Law, we also hear words of comfort and promise through the Messiah who would come.

Objectives

That the participant, led by the Holy Spirit through the Word, will

1. grow in his or her appreciation of the great treasure of salvation opened to us by the Key of David, Jesus, our Savior; and
2. do all he or she can in word and deed to share this precious hope with others.

Note for the small-group leaders: Lesson notes and other materials you will need begin on page 65.

For the Lecture Leader

Session Plan

Worship

Begin the session with the hymn and prayer printed in the study leaflet. Hymn accompaniments are available in denominational hymnals, such as *Lutheran Worship* (refer to hymnal index). (Note: Concordia Publishing House has available *Every Voice a Song*, a 9-CD set of organ accompaniments for 180 hymns and liturgy. All the initial worship hymns in the LifeLight courses are included in this resource. It's especially helpful for mission congregations and small parishes. See the list of study resources on page 7.)

Lecture Presentation

Introduction

Satan wanted to tidy up his arsenal and rearrange his weaponry so that his operation would run more smoothly. So he held a garage sale.

And as the story goes, a junior tempter arrived on the scene looking for some bargains. The tempter scrutinized the piles of temptations stacked up on hell's driveway and soon spotted a particularly well-worn missile.

"I notice," he said to the demon at the cash register, "that this . . . ah . . . item has no price tag."

"It's not for sale," came the reply.

"Everything's for sale. Everything has its price," said the cynical shopper.

"This weapon is not for sale," sneered the clerk. "This is our master's favorite. He's launched it with stunning effectiveness for centuries. He'll never give it up. Never."

Curious, the junior tempter walked over to where the weapon lay. He turned it over and read the label. Emblazoned on the missile in bold, black letters was the word *discouragement*.

How effectively has Satan lobbed this missile into your life in the past week or month? If you've found yourself reeling under the explosive power of its discharge, you're not alone. Most believers find themselves discouraged at one time or another. Some of us find ourselves there quite regularly.

Those in ancient Judah who truly loved their Lord and wanted to serve Him almost surely battled this same weapon. Put yourself in their place. Their society, as we have seen, had deteriorated. Everyone lived for themselves. Outwardly prosperous but spiritually bankrupt—that was the sad state of affairs in Judah.

Imagine hearing God's prophets warn and threaten God's punishment all to no avail. Imagine watching your culture crumble and then begin to collapse. We don't really have to strain too hard to imagine this scene. We recognize the symptoms of a sick society. We live in one. And our God knows it's easy to find ourselves discouraged and hopeless.

God knows. He truly does. God knew the situation of those in ancient Judah too. As we said last time, that's one reason Isaiah penned the Gentile oracles: to paint the big picture for God's people and comfort them with the truth that this sad state of affairs would not last forever. The wicked would come under God's judgment at last. Those—and only those—who would cling to Yahweh would escape that judgment. Such was their hope.

Important as that encouragement was for ancient Judah and as comforting as we find it for ourselves today, the Holy Spirit had a second purpose for these oracles as well. Through His prophet Isaiah, God's Spirit was calling the Gentile nations to repentance and faith too. God wanted them to share the hope of the Messiah, our Savior, Jesus Christ.

1 Nations Wait while God Watches (Isaiah 18)

And so, Isaiah 18 picks up where we left off last time: God's judgment on all nations. Before we can experience hope, we must see how hopeless our situation truly is. That's why Isaiah blasts the nations with the fiery message of coming judgment.

The oracle that began this week's readings is addressed to Cush. Some versions of the Old Testament translate this as Ethiopia. (Unlike Semites—including the Israelites—ancient Ethiopians and Egyptians were clean-shaven; see v. 2.) This region lies about as far from Jerusalem as the people of Isaiah's time could have imagined—the proverbial edge of the earth. Even there, God's judgment would fall.

Picture the scene the prophet paints in verses 3–4. The battle flag is raised. The trumpet sounds. God has the attention of the entire human family. Surely He will come with power and might! But God's response is simply one of quiet observation. Like dazzling heat whose presence is seen—even felt—as very near yet ever at a distance, so God waits for His time, His moment. Verses 5–6 tell us He will cut and prune, leaving the remains of human arrogance and ignorance for the birds and beasts.

And what is the final purpose of God's judgment? It is not simply to destroy, but to bring hope. He intends to gather a special people, His own people—a vinestock onto which He will graft individuals from all the nations of the earth. God will prune His vineyard. He will see to it that the vine grows healthily and bears abundant fruit.

Note (vv. 2, 7) that those who will bear the fruit are the very ones to whom Isaiah announced God's judgment. They will bring a gift to the Lord of hosts. Our Lord wants all people from every nation in every far-flung corner of the earth to recognize and repent of their sin and humbly come to God's presence.

In Isaiah's day, that presence was manifest in the temple that sat on the hill in Jerusalem called Mount Zion. Today, God manifests His presence wherever His Word is proclaimed. He manifests His presence whenever He touches people in the gracious waters of Baptism. He manifests His presence whenever He touches His children, strengthening them with Christ's precious body and blood in the Holy Supper.

2 The Burden against Egypt (Isaiah 19–20)

Mighty Egypt was the land of bondage, the land in which Israel suffered in slavery for four centuries. It had taken forty years for the sons of Israel to put Egypt behind them the first time. But this time, God comes quickly, riding on a swift cloud. Verse 1—Egypt's false gods will tremble. Verse 2—Egypt's citizens will turn against one another. Verses 5–8—The waters of the Nile will acknowledge the authority of the one true God. Those who had flaunted their authority as taskmasters over God's people will fall on their faces before the power of a greater Lord, a mighty King.

Isaiah does not identify the king described here (19:4). We know from other ancient sources that Egypt suffered internal strife, perhaps even civil war, during this time. The possibility that a tyrant would rise to power posed, no doubt, an ever-present threat. Isaiah, however, suggests that Egypt's greatest terror will come not from some recognized superpower but from little Judah instead.

The Lord of hosts, the mighty King of kings, had committed Himself to exercise the real power behind Judah's earthly, human throne. Egypt would be humbled, and its wisdom and might would wither. Egypt's help would prove a false hope as Egypt itself fell hopeless beneath the oppressor's boot.

But once again, God purposed not simply destruction but deliverance. God would come to strike and to humble, but also to save and heal. In an ironic twist, the great Egypt from whom God had rescued Israel would need rescuing too. And God would provide it. There was hope. God would send a Savior. Egypt would know the one true God just as God had promised Moses (Exodus 7:5). Egypt would worship (Isaiah 19:21) and would bring sacrifices and offerings.

For the exodus, God sent a deliverer named Moses (mÿshe in Hebrew). For the deliverance of the Egyptians, the Lord will send a mÿshía (Messiah).

Verses 23–25 add a twist to the prophecy. God not only brings salvation to the Egyptians, but now He adds the Assyrians! The warring nations give up their fight and worship together. The regions of Assyria and Egypt were among the first to convert to Christianity. Ironically, Jewish Christianity virtually disappeared by the second century. However, the ancient Coptic (Egyptian)- and Syrian (Assyrian)-speaking churches exist to the present day! The Lord has welcomed them to Zion as members of the new Israel—His Church.

In chapter 20, Isaiah showed Judah's people (20:1–4) the plain truth, the bare facts of their situation.

In the year (probably 711 BC) that an Assyrian army captured Ashdod, a city of Philistia, God told Isaiah to take off his usual prophet's clothes of sackcloth and walk about barefoot in only his loincloth undergarment. Why? Verses 3–6—This was an object lesson to Egypt and Cush (Ethiopia) that Assyria would "lead away the Egyptian captives and the Cushite exiles, both the young and the old, naked and barefoot, with buttocks uncovered, the nakedness of Egypt." Stripping captives of their sandals and outer garments was a common custom to shame a defeated nation. Verse 6—The object lesson was intended also as a warning to Judah.

3 The Burden against Babylon (Isaiah 21)

Now Babylon reappears on God's list of judgment. This time Babylon stands not as the archetypical enemy, but as merely one more false hope. Just as many in Judah had hoped for help from Egypt against Assyria, so many might have hoped that Babylon would serve as an ally from the east, one that would pressure and distract Assyria on its opposite border. But no help and no hope would come from Babylon either. Verse 11—Nor would Dumah (Edom) or (v. 13) Arabia in the south. None of the potential allies would be left standing in the withering heat of God's judgment. All our scheming will do is to keep us awake at night, waiting for the morning and hoping that the watchman will not need to shout warnings of danger or disaster.

Ancient Israel had several types of watchmen. During harvest time, watchmen were posted in the fields so that thieves would not steal the crops. Watchmen also patrolled city streets. Watchmen were positioned on the city walls, towers, and hills to detect troop movements by the enemy or to admit messengers. Isaiah refers to this last type of watchmen.

Edom would be destroyed and Arabia after it. But at the heart of Judah's false hope lay Babylon, and from the heart of chapter 21 rings out these fateful words (v. 9): "Fallen, fallen is Babylon." Babylon would fall. How true these words would prove when, in fact, some fifty years after Babylon destroyed Jerusalem, Elam, and Media, the great and mighty Babylon came crashing down itself.

4 The Burden in the Valley of Vision (Isaiah 22)

All of this brings Isaiah's burden very close to home. The mighty seer now focuses on his own people—a people with very poor spiritual insight. He somewhat sarcastically calls Jerusalem—a city situated on a hill surrounded by valleys—a valley of vision. Instead of a hill from which one can see what is coming, Jerusalem resembles nothing so much as a steep valley from which one can see very little.

Perhaps as an illustration, Isaiah points to Exhibit A (22:15–19): Shebna, the royal steward. His was a position similar, perhaps, to chief of staff or prime minister. He helped set policy. He controlled the king's agenda and scheduled his appointments. He held (22:22) the "key of the house of David" by deciding who would be admitted or excluded from the royal palace.

At this crisis in Judah's history, at this time when his

nation needed his leadership, support, wisdom, and guidance, Shebna used his position and power instead to complete a pet project. He built a grand tomb for himself! How ironic that he had resigned himself to his own death. How selfish that he thought only of memorializing himself in some monumental tomb instead of serving his king, his people, and above all, the King of kings.

Verse 17—Isaiah's words to Shebna predict not only a death without dignity, but also the disgrace of demotion. He would be deposed and replaced by Eliakim (see 36:22) on whom Judah's king and people would no doubt peg new hopes for national security. But Isaiah also sees the truth concerning Eliakim (vv. 23–25). Even a royal steward as committed to Judah as the faithful Eliakim would fail and fall. Those who lived in the valley so devoid of spiritual vision had created a burden of sin too heavy for any human leader to bear.

Yet a ray of hope shines through the darkness of this visionless valley. Eliakim, holding as he does the "key to the house of David" (v. 22), pictures the completely faithful servant whom God would send: Jesus.

This One would open and close the way of salvation. The key He holds unlocks the sealed door of sin (v. 14). When there seems to be no hope for forgiveness, the One who holds the key of David, the One who is Himself that key, comes. As we sing in Advent hymns, Immanuel has come to open wide our heavenly home by taking upon Himself our sin and guilt. His death has forced open the door to eternal life and guarantees that our iniquity has been forgiven.

5 The Burden against Tyre (Isaiah 23)

Finally, Isaiah unburdens himself of his last oracle. He once again focuses on Tyre. A seaport on the Mediterranean, Tyre was the doorway beyond which lay the ends of the earth. Thus the message is repeated yet one last time: the God of Judah rules the world, the heavens and earth, both land and sea. No one can escape His presence.

The word against Tyre is a word of judgment. A prosperous trade center, the city had stood from ancient times. Tyre had established many colonies around the Mediterranean world. News of her fall (vv. 5–6) would spread like waves on the water from Egypt to Tarshish, causing terror and dismay. If a cosmopolitan power like Tyre could fall, and with it much of the world's economy, then what security can this world offer?

None.

But for Tyre, as for all the other people Isaiah addressed in his oracles, hope lies in one direction: the God of Israel. Just as no one can escape His power or presence, so no one lives beyond His promise. As Judah's citizens would live in exile for seventy years, so Isaiah predicts (v. 15) a seventy-year captivity for Tyre also. But in the end, God will remember Tyre and bring the people back home.

Would they have learned their lesson? The final verses of the chapter leave some doubt. Verse 17—Many, it seems, will return to the ways of the old Adam.

So what are we to make of all this? Does despair have the final word after all? Not at all. The One who proclaims judgment on human sin is also the One who brings newness of life. God has taken the burden of human sin upon Himself. He has borne our griefs and carried the sorrows of every person of Adam's race.

22:14—Isaiah's words sting our ears: "Surely this iniquity will not be atoned for you until you die." Yet we can confidently reply that we have already died—died with Christ. We've been buried with Him in our Baptism, just as Romans 6 reminds us. We no longer stand outside God's kingdom. We no longer need to live as "strangers and foreigners," but we can live as "fellow citizens with the saints and members of the household of God" (Ephesians 2:19 NKJV).

No longer defined by external factors like our geographical birthplace or race or nationality, we are God's people. We belong to a kingdom that knows no geographic or political borders. This kingdom is found wherever God's people gather around His Word and the precious Sacraments. Empowered by Him through His means of grace, we await—in sure and certain hope—the day the key of David, our Immanuel, comes again.

Concluding Activities

Distribute the study leaflet for the next session. Close by praying together the last stanza of the hymn "Jesus Shall Reign" (*LW* 312).

In That Day

Isaiah 24–27

Preparing for the Session

Central Focus

Our Savior has defeated Satan and swallowed up the death we deserved because of our sin by absorbing the wrath of God in our place. He has planted us in His Church and enables us to bear abundant fruit. We praise Him now and into eternity.

Objectives

That the participant, led by the Holy Spirit through the Word, will

1. praise God for His victory over sin, Satan, and death;
2. bear abundant fruit, confident in the righteousness already his or hers in Christ; and
3. look forward with eagerness to the day in which Christ will come in all His glory to gather His people to live with Him forever.

Note for the small-group leaders: Lesson notes and other materials you will need begin on page 67.

For the Lecture Leader

Session Plan

Worship

Begin the session with the hymn and prayer printed in the study leaflet. Hymn accompaniments are available in denominational hymnals, such as *Lutheran Worship* (refer to hymnal index). (Note: Concordia Publishing House has available *Every Voice a Song,* a 9-CD set of organ accompaniments for 180 hymns and liturgy. All the initial worship hymns in the LifeLight courses are included in this resource. It's especially helpful for mission congregations and small parishes. See the list of study resources on page 7.)

Lecture Presentation

Introduction

An old cartoon pictures a robed man with a long beard marching up and down a busy street, carrying a sign on a pole. This sign reads, "Repent! The end is near!"

In the next frame the "prophet" has passed by, and we read the back side of his sign. It says, "If you already repented, disregard this notice."

Despite the nervous laughter, when God's people talk about Judgment Day, many folks can't quite snicker their fears away. Everyone wants fire insurance. Even those who don't believe in a divine day of reckoning find themselves drawn to movies or even lectures that claim to forecast the exact day our world will end or the events leading to Earth's destruction.

God's people probably view Judgment Day with a mixture of fear and joy. This world is, after all, the only reality we've ever known. We have plans for our own lives. We have hopes for the lives of our children or grandchildren. We don't want all this to come to a screeching halt. Not really. At least not yet.

On the other hand, we long for exactly that—for all this to come to an end. We long to see all wrongs put right. We long to see eternity dawn and watch sickness and sorrow dissolve like mist in the warm sunshine of God's love. We long to see death die and Satan's wretched schemes end.

The words of Isaiah 24–27, which you studied this past week, tell of the day that will happen. Maybe you noticed a critical phrase of three little words as you read: "In that day." These chapters give us a taste, a glimpse, of a reality beyond this world—a glimpse into the next.

People who are discouraged with their day-to-day lives sometimes ask, "Is this all there is?" Isaiah draws back the curtain that separates time from eternity. He lets us see for ourselves. He lets us hear our heavenly Father's answer to that question.

No.

This world is not the ultimate reality.

Sin's power is not the ultimate force in the universe.

Death—physical death—is not the ultimate end for My people.

Life—life on this planet—is not the sum total of My purpose for you.

Victory—victory over sin and Satan, hell and death—will ultimately be yours.

These are such powerful truths! Let's look at these texts more closely.

1 The Day of Judgment

Have you ever seen a high-tech slide show at a musum or on your computer? Images fade quietly in and out in seemingly random order. Perfectly synchronized and perfectly timed, such a presentation produces a powerful emotional effect.

A presentation like that resembles, in a way, Isaiah's approach in the chapters you read this week. His words project images into our minds and hearts in what has been called Isaiah's Apocalypse (chapters 24–27). The word *apocalypse*, as you saw in this week's assignments, carries the connotation of something that was once a mystery but has now been revealed. For example, it describes the Book of Revelation. (Perhaps you have even heard the expression "the four horsemen of the Apocalypse," a reference to Revelation 6:1–8.) Over time, the word *apocalypse* has come to mean not just any revelation, but the revealing of information about the last days in general and about Judgment Day in particular.

What will happen on the great Day of Judgment? The Holy Spirit through Isaiah reveals important details. Again and again in these chapters, we see the phrase "In that day."

- (24:1–4) In that day, God will empty the earth of its population and lay it waste.
- (24:7–13) In that day, God will change the world's joy and laughter to sorrow and tears.
- (24:19–20) In that day, God will destroy our very planet itself; it will reel, stagger on its axis, and split open.
- (24:21–22; 27:1) In that day, God will punish Satan and those who have by their attitudes and actions sworn allegiance to him.

What an awesome, even frightening, picture! No wonder the prophet Joel, when writing about this day, said, "The day of the LORD is great and very terrible" (Joel 2:11 NKJV).

Think of facing that day alone. Think of facing that day with no place of refuge, no protection, no protector, no Savior. Think of it, and then you will understand why our Lord Jesus quotes the people in that predicament on that day saying to the mountains, "Fall on us," and to the hills, "Cover us!" (Luke 23:30; see also Hosea 10:8; Revelation 6:16–17).

It will be a great and terrible day!

2 The Day of Salvation

Great for all, terrible for some, perhaps for most, but for us as God's children, the Day of Judgment turns out to be the Day of Salvation.

What will happen on that great day of salvation? The Holy Spirit through the prophet Isaiah reveals several details. Again we see the phrase repeated, "In that day."

- 25:9—In that day, the God for whom we have waited comes! We rejoice in His complete salvation. Here Isaiah adds a touch of vicious humor. In 25:9–12, he describes Moab trampled in manure as a symbol of the condemnation of the nations who resist the Lord. In 15:1–16:13, Isaiah had railed against Moab. The Moabites receive special attention because they are Israel's relatives as descendants of Lot (Genesis 19:36–37), but who constantly harassed Israel (e.g., 1 Samuel 14:47). God's hand of blessing comes to rest on Mount Zion, while Moab spreads out his hands in the dung "as a swimmer spreads his hands out to swim" (Isaiah 25:11).
- 26:1–6—In that day, God's people sing a song of peace, a song of security. We have become once more (v. 2) "the righteous nation that keeps faith."
- 27:2–6—In that day, God restores His vineyard, His Church; He protects it, waters it, tends it; and Israel, the

true people of God—that's us—blossom in the light of His love. We bear the fruit of faith in superabundance (27:6b).

• 27:12—In that day, God threshes His harvest field, gathering His precious children one by one. No one need fear being forgotten. No one need fear being left behind. Just as the blood marked the doorposts in ancient Egypt to tell the angel of death which houses and families to spare, so now the blood of Jesus marks each one of us. In our Baptism we have received the sign of the holy cross, the seal certifying us as God's own. As the apostle Paul promised centuries after Isaiah, "The Lord knows those who are His" (2 Timothy 2:19), and "The Lord will rescue me from every evil deed and bring me safely into His heavenly kingdom" (2 Timothy 4:18a).

Because we, like Paul, know this to be true, we join him in the prayer of praise that ends this part of his Letter to Timothy: "To [Christ] be the glory forever and ever. Amen" (4:18b).

• 27:13—In the day of salvation, the trumpet will sound, calling all God's people to worship Him. Our Lord's throne room will ring with the eternal, unending praise He rightly deserves for providing such a great salvation for us.

3 When Is This Day?

Maybe you have already guessed that there is no easy answer to that question, no quick three-word response. Instead, we ask, and we hear our Lord give us an answer summarized as, "Now and not yet."

When is this great and terrible day of the Lord? Surely we can see Good Friday as both great and terrible. On that day, our Lord Jesus hung and bled and died. He hung in my place. He bled in my place. He died in my place. And in yours. Theologians call this the *vicarious atonement,* and it is the greatest act of love history has ever seen. That day was terrible because of the terrible price our Lord Jesus paid and because of the crushing load of sin He bore.

But that day was great too, wasn't it? It was great in all our Lord accomplished, in all He won for us: forgiveness—of all sin; life—eternal life, a life that never, ever ends; and freedom—from the bondage, shame, pain, and frustration of life as Satan's slaves.

A great and terrible day, Good Friday.

But a great and terrible day stands on our horizon too. That day is about to dawn. You know the day I'm talking about—the day our Lord Jesus comes again to take all of God's scattered children home.

That day will dawn in darkness and terror for those who have rejected our God and His Christ. But even as the planet begins to break apart beneath our feet, we will—each one of us—find ourselves rising just as the apostle Paul says to "meet the Lord in the air, and so we will always be with the Lord" (1 Thessalonians 4:17). A great day! A day of salvation that will last forever. God, bring us to that endless day by Your great grace in Jesus Christ!

4 Living in the Now

The end of the world and Good Friday—both days are days of judgment and days of deliverance.

But before we close, we must consider one last great and terrible day. Remember that I said this day is both now and not yet? Before we leave, we need to look at the now part of that definition.

God's great and terrible day breaks in on His people each time He comes to us, each time He touches us through His Word and Sacrament. His holy touch is a terrible touch because it stirs up in our hearts recognition of our own unholiness. His Law demands repentance of us. And that process, the process of seeing our unrighteousness and our unloveliness, can be truly terrible.

But His touch is also great. It's great because it reminds us of His endless love for us. His Gospel supplies what His Law demands. His Word works true contrition, genuine sorrow, in our hearts for our sins. His Word assures us of our heavenly Father's complete forgiveness for all, each, and every one of those sins.

In the Lord's Supper, Jesus Himself touches our lips with His very own body and with His precious blood—the same body and blood that hung there on Calvary's cross to pay for our sin. What an awesome thing! What a great thing!

The great and terrible day of the Lord is Good Friday, when the Messiah hung, bled, and died for me and for you.

The great and terrible day of the Lord is each week in public worship, each day in our personal devotions, each time the Church celebrates the Sacrament, the body and blood of Christ for you.

The great and terrible day of the Lord is the day when the not yet becomes the now, the day the Lord Jesus comes with all His holy angels, the day the trumpet sounds and the dead are raised, and we are changed to live forever with the Lord. That is the great and terrible Day of the Lord.

Even so, come, Lord Jesus. Amen.

Concluding Activities

Distribute the study leaflet for the next session. Use 1 Thessalonians 5:23–24 as a closing benediction.

What Are You Waiting For?

Isaiah 28–30

Preparing for the Session

Central Focus

God's message to ancient Judah, like His message to us, never changes. He urges us to return to Him in repentance and faith so that in Christ He can forgive our sins and give us eternal life. He freely supplies all He demands. Even faith and repentance come to us as a gift. His faithfulness brings us hope and comfort.

Objectives

That the participant, led by the Holy Spirit through the Word, will

1. ask God to show him or her the hardness of heart, the spiritual blindness, that may be keeping him or her from seeing the truths of His Word;
2. cling to Jesus, the lion of Judah and the hearth of God, who endured the wrath of God in his or her place; and
3. look to the Lord as his or her only deliverer and source of peace, especially in times of difficulty.

Note to the small-group leaders: Leaders notes and other materials you will need begin on page 69.

For the Lecture Leader

Session Plan

Worship

Begin the session with the hymn and prayer printed in the study leaflet. Hymn accompaniments are available in denominational hymnals, such as *Lutheran Worship* (refer to hymnal index). (Note: Concordia Publishing House has available *Every Voice a Song,* a 9-CD set of organ accompaniments for 180 hymns and liturgy. All the initial worship hymns in the LifeLight courses are included in this resource. It's especially helpful for mission congregations and small parishes. See the list of study resources on page 7.)

Lecture Presentation

Introduction

Imagine yourself sitting in church this coming weekend. The sermon has begun, and it sounds strangely familiar. Imagine that after the first several sentences, you know for sure that your pastor is preaching the same sermon he preached last week. Suppose the following weekend the same thing happened. How many times in a row would you listen to the same sermon before you said something to your pastor about this?

And suppose that when you did comment, he said something like this: "I've noticed that people here don't pay much attention to sermons. They don't seem to hear what I say. At least, no one's life changes very much. When my people have acted on this sermon, I will get a new sermon."

Perhaps you noted something very much like this as you worked on this week's texts from Isaiah. Isaiah is still preaching the same sermon we heard back in chapters 1–12. We can guess why that is. God's people have not yet responded to His earlier warnings. They have not repented. That's why the Lord's message for them remains unchanged. What makes this all the more astounding is the fact that in the interim, Isaiah's messages have carried such potent threats (and such powerful promises).

As we saw in the Gentile oracles, the Lord does not wink at sin. He exacts a terrible penalty from impenitent sinners. Remember the wrath and destruction we talked about? God's Old Testament people heard those potent threats too. But sadly, most in Israel chose to ignore them.

They chose to ignore their role as well, the part God wanted them to play in bringing the Lord's Good News of the coming Savior to the nations. They could have been God's ambassadors, messengers of the King of kings! Instead, they sloughed off the honor of that and went on taking what security they could find or make for themselves—in silver and gold, in political alliances, in idol worship, in lying to themselves about the seriousness of the troubles they faced and the grossness of the sins they were committing.

God's Word hit a brick wall. Or more accurately, it hit the stony hearts of His people, hearts that were hardening more and more even as the prophet spoke.

Isaiah had, as we have seen, also preached some terrifying messages about the destruction not just of individual nations, but of the entire earth. Even so, God's people turned up their noses at the banquet their Lord promised to prepare for them in the face of their enemies. Their attitude seems to have been, "God won't judge us. He won't punish us. It will never happen here."

1 Woe to Ephraim (Isaiah 28)

So as we arrive at chapters 28–30, Isaiah has again turned his attention to God's own people in Judah and Jerusalem in particular. We see that chapter 28 addresses Ephraim, the Northern Kingdom. While it is difficult to date these chapters with certainty, it is possible that the Assyrians had not yet carried them away into captivity (722 BC). If so, Isaiah's message comes as the clanging of the last alarm bell they will ever hear; it warns of coming judgment.

It is just possible, though, that the Northern Kingdom has already fallen, and that Isaiah speaks these words to Judah rather than to Ephraim. Isaiah and the people may already have seen Samaria, the capital of the Northern Kingdom, fall. In that case, history, albeit recent history, would stand as a bloody, silent warning.

Whatever way we take it, we see clearly that Israel went on refusing God's gift of repentance and life to the bitter end. And their end was bitter. "What about you, Judah?" Isaiah asks. "In particular, what about the ways in which you are just like your sister Israel?"

Isaiah's questions sting as they ring out in chapter 28.

Verses 7–8—What about your drunkenness, your abuse of alcohol, the alcoholism among your so-called spiritual leaders?

Verses 9–13—What about your refusal to "hear the Word of God and keep it," your continuing rejection of the peace and rest that your Lord wants to give you?

Versus 10 and 13 make a play on words, repeating the same sounds in Hebrew. Isaiah may be mocking the stammering of the drunks he describes in verse 7 or mimicking the baby talk he refers to in verse 9. In verse 11, the sounds grow more serious. Following the exile, the Jewish religious leaders grew very sensitive about the preservation of the Hebrew language (Nehemiah 13:23–25), especially for use in worship. They described Hebrew as the tongue or language of the temple. The sound of foreign tongues was regarded as a threat of God's judgment. In 1 Corinthians 14:21–25, Paul applies Isaiah's words about the tongues of the Assyrians against church members at Corinth who insist on speaking in other languages during worship. Paul shows that neither national pride nor self-serving prayers should obscure the message of the Gospel for all nations and tongues.

Verses 14–15—What about your agreement with death, your false hope that you will be spared, your whistling in the approaching darkness of death, your blind refusal to accept the reality of the danger you have put yourselves in by your sin?

"Judah," Isaiah says in chapter 29, "you are just like Ephraim, only more so." And you will meet the same fate.

Verse 16—"Behold, I am the one who has laid as a foundation in Zion, a stone . . . a precious cornerstone." As we know from the New Testament (1 Peter 2:4–8), Isaiah here points to Christ, the coming Messiah, in whom alone there is hope. He is the cornerstone, the sure foundation of the Church—of all who trust in Him for salvation. But for those who reject Him, He becomes for them "a stone of stumbling" (1 Peter 2:8 and Isaiah 8:14).

2 Woe to Judah (Isaiah 29)

And that's where chapter 29 begins. It follows an outline very similar to chapter 28.

Verses 1–8—The threat of coming punishment (compare to 28:1–4).

Verses 9–16—The charges of drunkenness and stupefaction. Note this time it's not so much the abuse of alcohol the prophet addresses, but the people's spiritual stupefaction, their blind staggering and numbness to the truth that grows from their arrogant rejection of it (compare to 28:7–15).

Verses 17–24—God's promised marvelous or wonderful work, His work of rescuing those who returned to Him even while He destroys those who refuse His mercy and, in doing that, demand that He deal with them in judgment (compare to 28:16–29).

Law. Sin. God's call for repentance. Isaiah's message has not changed. The message has not changed because the people haven't changed. In fact, they have hardened their hearts still further until the Word of the Lord can scarcely penetrate it. It no longer moves them.

3 Woe to the Rebellious Children (Isaiah 30:1–14)

Rejecting God's wisdom, Judah found itself adrift on a sea of danger and confusion. The political situation grew steadily on toward night. The sounds of approaching battle roared in the ears of those now deaf to God's call for repentance and to His promise to help.

What to do? Where to go for security? You already know the decision Judah made. "We'll go back to Egypt," they said to one another. And so they did, forging a treaty that would bring them ruin. They forgot the four hundred years of miserable slavery their ancestors had endured at the hands of the Egyptians. They forgot the hardship and distress their nation had experienced there.

Egypt's help would bring only the disgrace of defeat. Egypt would prove to be a worthless ally (v. 7), as far as Judah's safety was concerned.

The Lord will give Judah what they say they want. They say to the prophets, God's spokesmen (vv. 9–11), "Don't see the truth. Don't tell the truth. And above all, for heaven's sake, get out of our way. Let us live our lives the way we want to live them. Stop bothering us with God's demands. We go to temple. We bring our offerings. We're there when He's told us to be. What more does He expect? What more can He want?"

They despised God's Word and the hearing of it. They despised God's Word and those who spoke it. And in the end, they got what they demanded. God did close the eyes of the seers (29:10). His Word became for His people a closed book, a sealed book, and His people became a nation of spiritual illiterates who couldn't make sense of the wisdom the Lord had so wanted to teach them.

4 Salvation in Repentance (Isaiah 30:15–33)

The same sermon again. And again. And again. God kept telling them, "In returning and rest you shall be saved; in quietness and in trust shall be your strength" (v. 15). But Judah would have none of it. Off she rode to round up help on her own (v. 16).

And so God waited. With infinite patience, He waited for His rebellious sons and daughters to wake up from their drunken stupor, to loathe the pigsty that had become their lives, to give up on their own ability to straighten out their lives, and to simply admit, "I can't do this on my own."

How is it with you? Are you waiting at your Lord's feet eager to hear His Word, eager to treasure it up in your heart, eager to put it to work in your life, and eager to let it do its softening, cleansing work in your heart?

Or is God waiting for you? Is He waiting for you to realize the truth of the words of "Rock of Ages, Cleft for Me"?

> Nothing in my hand I bring
> Simply to Your cross I cling. (*LW* 361)

Remember Ariel from chapter 29? *Ariel* means "the hearth of God." Jesus became God's hearth. Jesus took the heat of our sin—yours and mine—on Calvary's cross. He endured the furnace of God's wrath in our place.

Judah, like Israel before, would refuse to repent and would therefore experience the heavy hand of God's judgment. It need not have been that way. At Calvary, Jesus would pay the infinite price for Judah's sins. And because of Jesus, God could promise to restore all those of all time who would turn to Him in repentance and faith.

Robert Frost is credited with saying, "Home is the place where, when you have to go there, they have to take you in." Hearth and home—we need to go there. We long for our Father's welcome, our Father's table. We know we cannot claim that we deserve to come by any stretch of anyone's imagination.

But because of Jesus, God can take us in. Like the prodigal son in Jesus' story, we find a ready, happy welcome. The angels laugh with joy and sing praise to the God who receives sinners. Our heavenly Father spreads a banquet for us, just as we saw in the last session. God drapes Christ's own robe of righteousness over our shoulders. He slides a ring on our finger and gives us shoes for our feet—all these things as befitting the royal sons and daughters we have become in Christ.

The last half of Isaiah 30 depicts God's deep grace in even more detail. It rings with the blessings that belong to us, that belong to all of God's children in the now and in the not yet (but soon coming) future. You saw these as you did your study:

Verse 19—Our Father dries our tears and hears our cries for help.

Verses 20–21—Our Father directs our feet in the paths of righteousness—Christ's imputed righteousness—and in the right actions we want to do as our Father's children.

Verse 22—Our Father empowers us to throw out our idols and rely on Him alone.

Verses 23–26—Our Father supplies each and every one of our needs in abundance.

Verses 27–28—Our Father destroys our enemies and keeps us safe until He delivers His final decree of doom on them.

Verses 29–33—Our Father gives us gladness of heart, a song in the night, the sure and certain hope that day will soon dawn, the day of His ultimate victory when all wrongs are finally righted and all powers are securely and forever placed under His feet.

What are you waiting for? To hear and respond to God's Word? To welcome Christ at His return? To see the ultimate fulfillment of all your Savior's promises? If so, praise Jesus that He has worked these attitudes and this humility in you.

What is God waiting for? Your repentance, your return, your anxious, striving heart to become quiet enough to see the futility of your struggle to deliver yourself from the messes your sin has created? If so, don't prolong your agony. Don't harden your heart to His love for you. "Return to the LORD, your God, for He is gracious and merciful, slow to anger, and abounding in steadfast love" (Joel 2:13).

Concluding Activities

Distribute the study leaflet for the next session. Close by speaking the words of Paul's doxology from Romans 11:33–36 (printed in the study leaflet) aloud together. Encourage the group to speak the words slowly. Pause for a moment first and invite everyone to speak these words of worship from their hearts, hearts that have been cleansed and made new by the Holy One of Israel.

The King in His Beauty

Isaiah 31–33

Preparing for the Session

Central Focus

Israel's true King, Yahweh, is present in the midst of His people. As a holy God, He must punish the rebellion and sin of His people. Yet, in His mercy, God seeks to lead His people to repentance and trust in His forgiving love through the Savior He sends.

Objectives

That the participant, led by the Holy Spirit through the Word, will

1. state and explain the five major themes of Isaiah 1–33;
2. think through the implications of these major themes for his or her own life and the life of the Christian Church today;
3. thank God for making him or her part of His Church, His Zion; and
4. live secure in Christ's love, sharing the message of that love with others.

Note for the small-group leaders: Leaders notes and other materials you will need begin on page 72.

For the Lecture Leader

Session Plan

Worship

Begin the session with the hymn and prayer printed in the study leaflet. Hymn accompaniments are available in denominational hymnals, such as *Lutheran Worship* (refer to hymnal index). (Note: Concordia Publishing House has available *Every Voice a Song*, a 9-CD set of organ accompaniments for 180 hymns and liturgy. All the initial worship hymns in the LifeLight courses are included in this resource. It's especially helpful for mission congregations and small parishes. See the list of study resources on page 7.)

Lecture Presentation

Introduction

Have you ever attended a professional sporting event and then watched a sports report of that same event a few hours later? It's often fascinating to see a game that took two or three hours condensed into sixty seconds of highlights.

In some ways, it can be fun to see all the home runs or touchdowns or fumbles and foibles played back, one after the other. But it's not at all like seeing the game itself. Those who have not seen the plays that led up to the field goal can't appreciate the pressure on the fieldgoal kicker. Those who have not seen the action that preceded the three-error play really can't appreciate why the second baseman might have bobbled the ball so badly.

Being at the stadium, though, we do understand. And it makes the film clips of the sportscast that much more meaningful for us.

For the next few minutes, we're going to recap five essential points Isaiah has made in the first part of his Book. The verses from Isaiah you read for today highlight each of those points in a truly remarkable way. Because we've been at the stadium, so to speak, watching Isaiah minister to the people of Judah play by play, sermon by sermon, warning by warning, promise by promise, this recap will establish his message in our hearts in a way that wouldn't have been possible nine short weeks ago. If you answered questions 17 and 18 on your study leaflet, you've already begun to summarize for yourself the message Isaiah had for God's people seven hundred or so years before Christ was born. You've also begun to think through the meaning of that message for God's people today. Let's recap the highlights of that message in more depth together right now. What, in essence, did Isaiah say?

1 Yahweh Is Israel's True King

God's people had forgotten Him. They had ignored Him. They relied on the wisdom of their human king and on their king's diplomatic skills and political alliances. Still, Yahweh had not abandoned His throne.

Remember how this Lifelight course began back in Isaiah 1 and 6? Remember Isaiah's vision "in the year that King Uzziah died"? Remember the political unrest and international uncertainty Judah faced under the reign of the new king Jotham? Remember how Isaiah described the one he saw? "The King, high and lifted up!"

Uzziah had died, but Yahweh still sat enthroned above the roar of earthly battles, beyond the reach of earthly enemies. Yahweh reigned alive and well and ready to defend and care for His people.

This theme then—Yahweh, the true King—permeates Isaiah's Book. We've seen it from session 1 onward, and so it's no surprise that we see it in this week's readings as well. Listen, for instance, to these words (32:1, 18, 20):

> Behold, a king will reign in righteousness and princes will rule in justice. . . . My people will abide in a peaceful habitation, in secure dwellings, and in quiet resting places. Happy are you who sow beside all waters, who let the feet of the ox and the donkey range free.

2 God Is Present in the Midst of His People

From this picture and from the other pictures Isaiah paints of Yahweh's rule, we see that this glorious King is no despot. He cares deeply and desperately for His people. He reigns in justice. He gives peace to His people as He gathers them around Him in Zion. How blessed they truly are!

At the time Isaiah served God's people, they understood that God is present everywhere (omnipresent) in the same way we understand this divine attribute today. Still, the temple that stood on Mount Zion served as the unique place on earth where Yahweh met with His people. It was that place to which God's people came to worship Him and to enjoy His presence.

Isaiah prophesied of a time to come in which God would dwell among His people as Immanuel—God with us. As New Testament Christians, we recognize our Lord Jesus as the fulfillment of Isaiah's Immanuel prophecies. We see Jesus as the true messianic King who will sit on the throne of His father David forever.

Isaiah 33 describes the immediate historical events of the prophet's own lifetime. Yet features of the passage also anticipate the coming messianic age. The following passage and image help explain this aspect of biblical prophecy—how to interpret and apply it. The Bible doesn't read like an encyclopedia. Often the writers of Scripture present the workings of God like pictures of a landscape. In a landscape you might have some trees in the foreground, some animals grazing off in the distance, and a huge mountain looming in the background. Many miles separate the objects in the scene, yet all of the objects appear right next to each other on the picture's surface. In a similar way, a single section of Scripture often shows numerous events separated from one another, not by space but by time. From our perspective the events can seem unrelated. To make sense of these pictures in Scripture, we must consider what connects the different events. In the foreground is the punishment of Judah and Jerusalem; in the distance is the restoration of Zion; and in eternity are the blessings of Zion, the fullness and peace of God's kingdom in heaven.

As New Testament believers, we recognize that still today God calls and gathers His people around Himself. But God has not tied His presence to any specific geographical location like Zion. Rather, He has tied Himself to His people in His Word and Sacraments.

Wherever His Word is preached, our King is there. Remember what Jesus said (Matthew 18:20)? "Where two or three are gathered in My name, there am I among them."

Wherever the Holy Sacraments are celebrated, there our Lord meets with us. There He touches us by water, His Word, and in His body and blood in, with, and under bread and wine.

In ancient Judah, God was present in the midst of His people. In Toronto and Memphis, Maine and Oregon, Dallas and Minneapolis, Fort Leonard Wood and (name your state, province, town, or city here), God is still present in Zion, in the midst of His people. He is present to comfort, forgive, help, and deliver gifts through Word and Sacrament. Remember those comforting words from this week's readings? They point us to His help now and to the final victory in heaven.

3 God's Presence Is a Two-Edged Sword

How glad God's people feel in His presence! But still, how fearsome that presence becomes at times. We have seen how Jerusalem became God's hearth, the place where the fierce heat of His judgment fell because of His people's sins. Who in our group today can fail to join the "sinners in Zion" (33:14) when they cry out, "Who among us can dwell with the consuming fire? Who among us can dwell with everlasting burnings?"

Throughout the Book of Isaiah our Lord has revealed Himself as "the Holy One of Israel." Our God is, indeed, a merciful God. But He is also a God of justice, a God who hates sin and who must punish it, a God whose very nature keeps Him from overlooking even the slightest infraction, even the smallest act of disobedience.

We saw this in Isaiah's first encounter with the Holy One. Remember Isaiah's words (6:5)? "Woe is me! For I am lost; for I am a man of unclean lips, and I dwell in the midst of a people of unclean lips; for my eyes have seen the King, the LORD of hosts!"

That was the first time we heard Isaiah pronounce that word *woe*, but it surely wasn't the last. We heard him speak words of woe and warning against Judah again and again in chapters 2–12. Then we heard him repeat it again as he preached the Gentile oracles in chapters 13–23. What heavy burdens he proclaimed against Babylon, Assyria, Philistia, Moab, Egypt, and all the rest.

Instead of becoming lighter, Isaiah's burden grew heavier still (chapters 24–27) as he preached of the woe that was to come upon the peoples of the whole earth because of their rebellion, sin, and wickedness.

The Book of Isaiah has been called by some "The Letter to the Romans of the Old Testament." It's little wonder. The apostle Paul uses words and pictures much like those of Isaiah before him to strip everyone—those inside Israel and those outside alike—of every vestige, every thread, of self-righteousness. Remember Paul's words? (Romans 1:21–22; 28–2:1)

For although they knew God, they did not honor Him as God or give thanks to Him, but they became futile in their thinking, and their foolish hearts were darkened. Claiming to be wise, they became fools. . . .

Since they did not see fit to acknowledge God, God gave them up to a debased mind to do what ought not to be done. They were filled with all manner of unrighteousness, evil, covetousness, malice. They are full of envy, murder, strife, deceit, maliciousness. They are gossips, slanderers, haters of God, insolent, haughty, boastful, inventors of evil, disobedient to parents, foolish, faithless, heartless, ruthless. Though they know God's decree that those who practice such things deserve to die, they not only do them but give approval to those who practice them.

Therefore you have no excuse, O man, every one of you who judges. For in passing judgment on another you condemn yourself, because you, the judge, practice the very same things.

4 God Restores His Repentant People

This was not a pretty picture. Not in ancient Judah. Not in the world outside Judah in Isaiah's time. Not in our world today. And, truth be told, the picture is seldom a pretty one inside the visible Church today.

Still, Paul's words ring true today, both inside and outside Zion: "Therefore you have no excuse." God's people still echo Isaiah's words (Isaiah 6:5): "Woe is me! For I am lost; for I am a man of unclean lips, and I dwell in the midst of a people of unclean lips; for my eyes have seen the King, the LORD of hosts!" But even as God gives us His gift of contrition (and contrition truly is His gift), and even as God works in us His gift of repentance (and repentance truly is His work), even so He fulfills His promise to restore and cleanse us.

Still today God urges us to come to Him, promising us that (30:15) "In returning and rest you shall be saved; in quietness and in trust shall be your strength."

Still today God comforts His children with the Good News of our righteousness, of our right standing before our Father. God's servants soothe our troubled hearts with words like those He spoke through Isaiah long ago (3:10): "Tell the righteous that it shall be well with them, for they shall eat the fruit of their deeds." We can rely on our God's gracious promise that (33:24) "the people who dwell [in Zion] there will be forgiven their iniquity."

And so, those who dwell in Zion, live in peace. We live in true security with the Holy One of Israel as our defender, as our refuge from any storm, any danger, any fear. You remember some of the beautiful pictures of that security Isaiah painted for us as we went along, don't you? The chapters that we read this past week include portraits of that deep peace and security. Remember this one (33:17, 20–22)?

> Your eyes will behold the king in His beauty; they will see a land that stretches afar. . . . Behold Zion, the city of our appointed feasts! Your eyes will see Jerusalem, an untroubled habitation, an immovable tent, whose stakes will never be plucked up, nor will any of it cords be broken. But there the LORD in majesty will be for us a place of broad rivers and streams, where no galley with oars can go, nor majestic ship can pass. For the LORD is our judge; the LORD is our lawgiver; the LORD is our king; He will save us.

5 God's People Are Witnesses to All Nations

Forgiveness. Peace. Security. Strength.

Confidence. Joy. Righteousness. None of us have unwrapped every last package our heavenly Father wants to give us. None of us have fully studied and experienced all His gifts. How generous His heart! How limitless His goodness toward His children! Our wonder and our worship need have no limits either.

In Zion, and only in Zion, our God continues to fling His heart open wide to present to us, His unworthy creatures, the infinite riches His Son purchased for us with His own blood.

These treasures are beyond any shadow of doubt worth sharing! And that's just what the people of Zion want to do best—share the treasure of salvation with all nations.

Gathered in the light, gathered around the Holy One, Zion shouts to those still in darkness (2:3): "Come, let us go up to the mountain of the LORD, to the house of the God of Jacob."

We plead with the people of a world that is even now dying and slipping into the nighttime of an eternal hell (31:6), "Turn to Him from whom people have deeply revolted."

We say to those who live in open rebellion against God (33:13), "Hear, you who are far off, what I [God] have done." We plead with those who live within the shadow of the visible Church but who continue to deny God's claim on their lives, "and you who are near, acknowledge [His] might."

And as we plead and pray, we wait. We wait—but not for Judgment Day. We've already experienced that. We died with Christ as God's judgment struck Calvary's mountain centuries ago. We were buried with Christ as the holy waters of Baptism touched our bodies and our heavenly Father placed His mark of ownership on us. We arose with Christ as He left the tomb, forever after immune to any of the threats death can hurl at the unrighteous.

Now crucified with Christ and raised with Him, we await His eternal feast of victory even as we celebrate the feast of victory wherein death was swallowed up for us through the very body and blood of Christ given and shed for us. We live with both feet in the reality of the present, but we long for the fullness of salvation that is not yet revealed in us. We await our Lord's return in glory to gather His people around Him in Zion. In the peace that surpasses all human understanding, we await the peace that will never pass away. We await the return of Zion's true and only Savior.

The Lord is our Judge. The Lord is our Lawgiver. The Lord is our King. It is He who will save us. Even so, come, Lord Jesus! Amen.

Concluding Activities

Speak the words of stanza 4 of today's hymn as your closing prayer of praise. Point out that it is a doxology, expressing our adoration and worship to the triune God, Father, Son, and Holy Spirit. Make any necessary announcements, including information about the next LifeLight course.

Small-Group Leaders Material

Isaiah, Mighty Seer

Isaiah 1, 6, and Related Historical Texts

Preparing for the Session

Central Focus

As we begin this study of Isaiah, we meet its author. We set the social, political, and spiritual stage for the Book as we probe conditions in the nation of Judah in the seventh century before Christ. We also catch a glimpse of God's glory as He reveals Himself to Isaiah and calls him into the prophetic office.

Objectives

That the participant, led by the Holy Spirit through the Word, will

1. understand the political, social, and spiritual scene into which God sent Isaiah as His spokesman;
2. comprehend Isaiah's message as one of both sin and grace, Law and Gospel;
3. realize that the message of repentance and forgiveness that Isaiah spoke to God's Old Testament people is the same message our Lord speaks to us today;
4. respond to that message in humble confession and confident peace, assured that his or her sins are forgiven for Jesus' sake.

For the Small-Group Leader

Small-Group Discussion Helps

Day 1 • Introduction

1. Clues are provided in 2 Chronicles 26:1–15. (a) King Uzziah led his country to steady prosperity and this led people to feel satisfied with their political leader. The nation's economy blossomed. The king set agricultural policies that encouraged rural development. It would seem from the text that he himself employed many agricultural workers on his own farms and in his own vineyards (vv. 4–5, 10). The text gives no hint that the king's military adventures upset his citizens. In fact, the victories cited in the text probably fanned the fires of patriotism. The tribute Uzziah collected from the peoples he conquered probably served to keep taxes lower at home. These factors increased the king's popular support (vv. 6–8). Finally, the king's building projects probably kept unemployment low and pleased the civic-minded citizens, at least in the towns and villages in which they were carried out (vv. 9–10). (b) Let participants share their thoughts. The people of Judah might have felt anxious about the same things we would under similar circumstances. What new economic policies will the new king institute? Will taxes go up? Will I still have a job if the tower-building or well-digging projects, now supported by the government, are discontinued? Accept other reasonable responses the group mentions.

2. (a) Typically, the attitudes of the leaders in ancient Israel reflected the attitudes of the people. But we see Uzziah acting unfaithfully. In contrast, the priests endeavor to follow God's Word and so oppose the king. (b) The king's reckless attempt to assume duties God had reserved only for the priests hints at the pride and lust for power that lay buried just below the surface of his heart. The old saying "A river can't rise above its source" has application here. With a leadership committed to personal power and neglect or deliberate disobedience of God's holy Law, the people were likely to develop a similar attitude of impiety.

3. As time permits, allow volunteers to read their summaries of Jotham's reign. Move quickly into (b). Jotham apparently learned to respect the boundaries of power and privilege the Lord had erected around the Old Testament priesthood and the priestly sacrifices. However, the people continued to act with disregard for the laws of God.

4. Again, allow time for volunteers to read their summaries or examples from their list.

5. *For personal reflection. Sharing optional.* Point out that it's easy to complain, "Ain't it awful?" as we think about

all the corruption in the society around us. Those in seventh-century Judah might have played that game too. This question, however, may point out ways we may see ourselves trapped in Judah's sins. Ask if this was true. (a) Assure the group that you will not ask them to reveal the items they marked on their lists. But do ask whether or not they found it easy or difficult to identify with the sins the people of Judah were committing at the time of Isaiah's ministry. (b) Let volunteers share the comfort they found in this verse of Gospel.

Day 2 • Isaiah 6:1–7

6. (a) Move quickly around the group as each person shares the words he or she chose. (b) Accept any answers that come from the text itself. Isaiah says he saw the Lord, but he never describes the Lord. He focuses on the seraphim and signs of God's presence. (c) Again, accept responses that come directly from the text.

7. (a) Seeing God's majesty and hearing the worship offered by the angels, Isaiah found himself overwhelmed by his own sinfulness. He responded by confessing his own sin and the sins of his nation. (b) In contrast to our own culture in which people most often see themselves as individuals, Isaiah's confession reflects the more scriptural view of society. We belong to one another. Each of us contributes to the whole. To be sure, we retain individual responsibility for the direction of our own lives, but we also share jointly in the responsibility for the direction our society takes.

8. The words *unclean lips* probably refer to the hypocrisy and lack of integrity by which both Isaiah and the other citizens of Judah had offended the Lord. (a) Isaiah 29:13 refers to this. With their lips, God's people said the right things. Their actions, however, betrayed the evil that lay buried in their hearts. (b) God assured the prophet of His full and free forgiveness. He sealed the words of that Absolution with the burning coal taken from the altar. (c) Since Isaiah would use his mouth to speak God's Word, this action tied as it was to the spoken Absolution would have comforted Isaiah. God promised that the prophet's lips had been cleansed for the holy work they were to do.

9. *For personal reflection. Sharing optional.* Move on to 10 unless someone volunteers an observation.

Day 3 • Isaiah 6:8–13

10. Isaiah speaks the stirring words "Here am I. Send me!"

11. Responses will vary, but may well include "keep on hearing, but do not understand"; "keep on seeing, but do not perceive"; "the heart of this people dull"; "their ears heavy and blind their eyes"; "cities lie waste without inhabitant"; "the houses without people and the land is a desolate waste"; "the LORD removes people far away, and the forsaken places are many in the midst of the land"; and "[The land] will be burned."

12. *For personal reflection. Sharing optional.* If volunteers want to share, allow them (as time permits). You might also (or instead) ask group members to comment on when this is true of believers in general.

13. (a) Verse 13 speaks about "the holy seed," the few faithful believers that would be left in Judah. From this seed, the nation would again sprout. (b) Let participants share their favorite words of the grace God promises to repentant sinners.

Day 4 • Isaiah 1:1–20

14. (a) Isaiah 1 has so many pictures that it is unlikely that anyone will find them all. Here are some of the more prominent word pictures the prophet paints: The people have turned their backs on the Lord (v. 4); they are bruised, bloodied, beaten, and sick with sin (v. 5); the nation is burned, pillaged, and looted (v. 7); the people are as deserted as a hut built for temporary shelter in a melon (or cucumber) field (v. 8); they trample God's house, making an unwelcome mess when they come to worship (v. 12); their hands are bloody (v. 15); the nation that was to have been God's bride has become a prostitute instead (v. 21); the nation that was as precious as silver is now worthless (v. 22); and the nation whose love for God had the full-bodied bouquet of a choice wine is now watery, weak, and worthless (v. 22). Accept other responses drawn from the text. (b) Let volunteers share their thoughts.

Day 5 • Isaiah 1:21–31

15. (a) Again, let participants share their thoughts. Remember that an idol is anything or anyone (other than the Lord) from which we hope to gain good or to which we turn for help in times of harm and danger. Here are examples of idolatrous doctrines/thoughts: "Christ is just one path to God"; "God will eventually save all people, no matter what they do or believe"; and "Religion is so personal that it's not proper for me to share my beliefs with others." (b) In Christ, God has declared us to be righteous and faithful (v. 26). He confirmed His promise to Israel by raising Christ from the dead. He confirms forgiveness to all through the cleansing of Holy Baptism. We have been redeemed by God's amazing sacrifice of His one and only Son. Together with the psalmist we can say, "If You, O LORD, should mark iniquities, O Lord, who could stand? But with You there is forgiveness, that You may be feared" (Psalm 130:3–4).

The Day of the LORD

Small-Group Leaders Session 2

Isaiah 2–5

Preparing for the Session

Central Focus

In these chapters, Isaiah confronts God's people with their sins of pride and idolatry. He unmasks their smug self-satisfaction and describes the coming "day of the LORD," the day of God's judgment and wrath.

But God's prophet also preaches the Gospel, saying, "Come, let us go up to the mountain of the LORD . . . that He may teach us His ways and that we may walk in His paths" (Isaiah 2:3).

Objectives

That the participant, led by the Holy Spirit through the Word, will

1. see clearly the implications of God's wrath and judgment on human sin;
2. identify in Judah's sins of pride and idolatry his or her own rebellion and disobedience;
3. receive the grace and goodness of God in His forgiveness won for him or her by the "branch of the LORD," our Savior, Jesus; and
4. grow a life of fruitfulness as he or she continues to "abide in the vine," drawing strength from Him.

For the Small-Group Leader

Small-Group Discussion Helps

Day 1 • Read Isaiah 2:1–4

1. (a) To walk in the Lord's paths primarily means to serve and trust in Him. As His Spirit leads us to know Him better, we grow more and more like Him. We learn His ways of Law and Gospel. (b) Transformation happened in the same way under the old covenant as it happens under the new covenant—by God's grace. He must call, lead, and teach us. He must strengthen us to walk in His paths and even give us the desire to do that. Careful study of the text shows God taking the initiative in each case: Isaiah 2:3—He will teach us His ways, and then we shall walk in His paths; Genesis 17:1—God chose and called Abraham, His servant; Psalm 86:11—He teaches us His way, and then we will walk in His truth; and Psalm 143:8–10—He shows us the way and teaches us to do His will.

2. (a) God's Old Testament people first went to the tabernacle and later to the temple on Mount Zion (Jerusalem), the places God had set aside to meet with His people. (b) Today God meets with His people as they gather together around His Word and the Sacraments. Rather than referring to a specific geographic place, the "mountain of the Lord's house" and the other terms used in this text refer to God's presence, particularly as He "calls, gathers, and sanctifies" His Church, His family that joins together for worship and for the ministry of the Word and Sacrament. (c) The cross of Jesus Christ stands as the focal point of all history. It stands as a beacon of God's love, as a magnet that draws the hearts of people to Him through repentance and faith in His Word. In a very real sense, the "mountain of the Lord" is and ever will be the hill outside Jerusalem, where the Savior bled and died for us sinners.

3. (a) Jews and proselytes (Gentile converts) from all over the ancient world gathered to hear God's Word at the temple in Jerusalem. Through Peter's Pentecost sermon, they learned that Jesus of Nazareth was the Messiah. (b) Still today, God continues to draw people to Himself in Christ. He will continue to do that until time ends. In fact, that's the reason time continues—to give more people time to repent and believe the Gospel (2 Peter 3:9).

4. (a) Jesus did not promise earthly peace. Rather, He warned of continuing wars and rumors of wars. He assured His listeners that these conflicts would continue until His return to judge the earth. Even though many Christians have fallen into the belief that the

verses in Isaiah refer to earthly peace, this cannot be true. Scripture does not contradict itself. Jesus did not contradict Isaiah. Therefore, those who seize upon Isaiah 2:4 as a promise of eventual nuclear disarmament and the disbanding of all earth's standing armies will find themselves sorely disappointed. (b) When we read Jesus' promises of peace (John 14) together with the promises of peace described by Isaiah, we hear the strains of both songs blend in perfect harmony. God's people will enjoy the fullness of His peace in our heavenly home. There all conflict will have ceased. All of heaven's citizens will live in complete love and unity. Even now we can live in the hope of God's peace through our relationship with Jesus Christ. Forgiven in Him, we enjoy peace with God, and we can draw on His power to live at peace with those around us (Romans 5:1ff).

5. *For personal reflection. Sharing optional.* Move on to the next question.

Day 2 • Read Isaiah 2:5–22

6. Verse 5 adds the thought of walking in the light of the Lord. Psalm 119:105 explains that God intends His Word to be a lamp for our feet and a light for our path. God's people were not walking in His light at the time Isaiah wrote. This verse links the picture of promised peace (Isaiah 2:1–4) with the picture of prideful idolatry Isaiah paints next.

7. God's people are full of superstitions from the East. Their land is full of silver and gold. There is no end to their treasures. Their land is full of horses. There is no end to their chariots. Their land is full of idols. The items mentioned represent wealth because they were not essential for daily living (e.g., horses were used for war and military parades, not daily transportation).

8. (a) Rather than consult God, the people turned to Egypt. (b, c) *For personal reflection. Sharing optional.* Do not ask participants to share their answers. (d) As we confess our sins of pride and idolatry and as we ask our Lord for help in overcoming them, He grants us His forgiveness. With His Absolution, He gives us His power to overcome the sins in our lives. It's especially important to gather regularly with other believers to hear the Good News of God's forgiveness and to share His peace with each other.

Day 3 • Isaiah 3–4

9. (a) Let the group share its responses. Accept any threat that comes from the text. (b) Again, share examples with one another. Note that 3:14–15 expresses God's anger at Judah's leadership. (c) God has given those in spiritual leadership an awesome privilege, but also an awesome responsibility (see Titus 1:6–9), which is all the more reason for us to pray for those whom God has placed in spiritual authority over us. (d) We are to pray for them and support them in the work God has given them to do in His name and for the sake of us all.

10. Answers will vary. Emphasize the role of organized study, prayer, and devotion.

11. (a) Isaiah 3:18–23 lists twenty-one material blessings that the proud and impenitent cherish. God will snatch all of these away. (b) **Challenge question.** God will remove completely (3 x 7) the riches and status symbols in which the people take pride.

12. (a) In these verses, God promises to send the branch—the Messiah. The land will again produce spiritual fruit, lush and beautiful. (b) God's people—the true believers, Zion, the "everyone who has been recorded for life in Jerusalem"—will be washed of the filth of their sin. God will protect, comfort, and hide them from all danger. His peace will be theirs forever in heaven.

Day 4 • Isaiah 5:1–7

13. (a) The Lord gave His vineyard all the care He possibly could. He did for His people everything He could have done to ensure their fruitfulness. This is stated symbolically in Isaiah's song in terms like "cleared it of stones," "planted it with the choicest vines," "built a watchtower," and "hewed out a wine vat." (b) There can be no good reason for the unfruitfulness of His vineyard, His people. They, like we, have no excuse for the sin in their lives.

14. Scripture never tells us to try harder to produce the fruit of the Spirit. Rather, it points us to Christ and to a deeper union with Him. As we remain united to the vine, we receive the nutrients we need to produce spiritual fruit.

Day 5 • Isaiah 5:8–30

15. (a) Isaiah gives these examples: greed and selfishness (v. 8), sensuality and drunkenness (vv. 11–12), deliberate rebellion and blaspheming God's grace (vv. 18–19), distorting the truth and denying the relevance of God's commands (v. 20), self-centered pride (v. 21), boasting about sin rather than repenting for it (v. 22), and injustice (v. 23). (b) The latter examples listed here show that something more had gone wrong. The people mock God's justice and overturn goodness. They reject and despise the Word.

16. (a) Few people in our culture would categorize any of these things as heinous crimes. (b) Most people in our culture would probably label the sins on the list as petty and inoffensive and even claim some of them as their civil rights. (c) This calls for a personal response from participants. Let volunteers respond.

17. (a) God's arm is stretched out, ready to fall in judgment on the sinful and impenitent. (b) Judgment has not yet fallen; His arm is still outstretched. In grace, God gives us time to acknowledge our sin and to come to Him to receive mercy and grace. The final blow was yet to come—the one that fell on Jesus. The judgment would grow still worse, but our Savior would receive that judgment for us.

Oh, Come, Oh, Come, Immanuel!

Small-Group Leaders Session 3

Isaiah 7:1–9:7

Preparing for the Session

Central Focus

Isaiah wrote eloquently about the sign of Immanuel. This promise from God was for ancient Judah what it is for us today—a two-edged sword. Jesus is our Immanuel.

Objectives

That the participant, led by the Holy Spirit through the Word, will

1. understand the sign of Immanuel as both God's Word of Law and His Word of Gospel to His people;
2. repent for trying to take the responsibility for his or her salvation into his or her own hands;
3. give praise to Jesus, our Immanuel, for the complete deliverance He has earned for us.

For the Small-Group Leader

Small-Group Discussion Helps

Day 1 • Isaiah 7:1–9

1. Ask participants to identify the characters named on their study leaflet. Accept reasonable answers, such as these: Ahaz—king of Judah (Southern Kingdom), grandson of Uzziah, son of Jotham; Rezin—king of Syria who joined forces with Israel to attack Judah; Pekah—king of Israel (Northern Kingdom) who formed an alliance with Rezin against Judah in an attempt to avoid being invaded and plundered by Assyria; and Shear-jashub—son of Isaiah whose name means "a remnant shall return" and who went with Isaiah to confront Ahaz at the aqueduct in Jerusalem.

2. Ahaz is inspecting one of Jerusalem's aqueducts in preparation for the siege that he knows is imminent. Apparently Syria and Israel have invaded Judah and captured other strategic cities. It appears so from the fact that Ahaz is even now taking precautions against a direct assault on the capital itself.

3. (a) God gave names both to comfort and, at times, to warn His people. The names were undoubtedly a constant reminder to those named of God's purpose in their lives. (b) The boy was named as a sign and portent of what God would do in Israel.

4. (a) God takes the initiative. He comes to us when we have no desire or power to seek Him out. He is a compassionate, loving God, deeply concerned about His people and our needs. (b) Syria and Ephraim boast that they will raze Judah's defenses and depose Ahaz, replacing him with their puppet—the son of Tabeel. God says that together Syria and Israel amount only to smoldering stubs. Their threats will turn out to be meaningless. As history records, God's Word about this situation came true. In 732 BC, Syria's capital Damascus fell to the Assyrians. In that same year, so did Israel. They would threaten Judah no longer. (c) *For personal reflection. Sharing optional.* If time will allow and individuals want to comment on what they see happening in general among human beings, invite them to do so. Stress, however, the main point: God's continuing, steadfast love despite His people's faithlessness. He still draws us to Himself in repentance and faith. He sends people to speak His Word to us and to warn us of our sin and remind us of our Savior. The words of 2 Timothy 2:13 come to mind: "If we are faithless, He remains faithful—for He cannot deny Himself." (d) Our heavenly Father did not withhold His only Son, but gave Him up to death on the cross for our sins. That sacrifice erases the debt we owe God because of our sins. The cross and the enormity of the sacrifice God made there can also help assure our hearts that God will not withhold any other good thing from us. If our hearts wonder whether or not we can trust our God, we need only look at the cross. What more powerful answer could God have provided?

Day 2 • Isaiah 7:10–25

5. God wanted Ahaz to trust Him. In addition to a word of promise, God binds that promise to something Ahaz could see and touch. Remind the group that God still does that today in Baptism and in the Holy Supper.

6. Ahaz found himself backed into a corner. If he asked for a sign, he would have to heed the sign, and Ahaz was not ready to trust God to handle this situation for him.

7. Answers will vary, depending on whether participants focused on the virgin, on the child, or on the name of the child. All are significant. The fact that the child would be born of a virgin suggests that this would ultimately be no ordinary birth. Matthew makes it clear that the virgin birth of Jesus is the fulfillment of the prophecy. (Some scholars suggest that a child was born naturally to one who was still a virgin when Isaiah first spoke these words.) The child, of course, would be the sign that God does deliver on His promise, that what His people wait for in faith will, in fact, come to be. Perhaps most significant in this sign is the name of the child: *Immanuel*, "God with us." The sign is an earthly, tangible, real bit of evidence of God's very presence in the midst of His people.

8. (a) Ahaz turned to the Assyrians and formed an alliance with them for protection. (b) Ahaz's plan to defuse and defeat the northern coalition by means of his treaty with Assyria would backfire and blow up in his face. In fact, Assyria did defeat Judah's enemies and crushed the threat they posed to Judah in 732 BC. (The complete destruction of Israel did not come until 722 BC.) But the Assyrian army had no intention of stopping at Judah's border. They would continue to march toward Jerusalem, leaving the country as desolate as though it were shaved bare by the razor of Assyria.

9. (a) **Challenge question.** Today the water of Baptism and the bread and wine of the Lord's Supper serve as visible, tangible signs of our Lord's presence among us. (b) *For personal reflection. Sharing optional.* As time will permit, let volunteers share their thoughts.

Day 3 • Isaiah 8:1–10

10. (a) Isaiah was confident that God, who had revealed His plan to save Judah, would deliver on His Word. (b) *Maher-shalal-hashbaz* is Hebrew for "quick to the plunder, swift to the spoil." The interpretation in verse 4 suggests that this name referred to the fact that the northern coalition would quickly become booty, despoiled by Assyria.

11. (a) The peaceful waters of Shiloah contrast sharply with the tsunami that was Assyria. Suggest to participants that God's promised peace flows from unexpected sources: a gentle stream that carries little power, such as the Word of promise that leaves Ahaz wanting something more. What Ahaz sought was the great power and might of Assyria that would now come like a great wave and destroy the northern coalition. But it would keep coming like flood waters out of control and overflow from Israel right on to Judah, even to the doorstep of Jerusalem. (b) The water in a baptismal font is gentle and quiet, but it carries God's divine power. It saves by destroying—drowning—the old Adam of sin and death. (c) *For personal reflection. Sharing optional.* Encourage participants who did not give much thought to this question to do so during the coming week. It's important to stress that we cannot change our indifference in spiritual matters by simply trying harder to care more about the things of God. We need to repent—to confess our sin, to ask for God's mercy and forgiveness, and to rely on Him to change our hearts and minds. He's promised to do that, and we can trust His Word to us.

Day 4 • Isaiah 8:11–22

12. (a) Answers will vary. These verses appear to be directed primarily at Isaiah himself. (b) Remind participants that Isaiah's message must have sounded like utter folly to his listeners. Since Isaiah had disapproved of the king's plan, perhaps those who supported Ahaz accused Isaiah of conspiracy or even of treason. The Lord wanted to assure and comfort His prophet. (c) *For personal reflection. Sharing optional.* Invite comments from volunteers as time will allow. (d) Isaiah responds to the threat by trusting God and by obeying His counsel to fear God alone. Then he seems to have gone on his way somewhat quietly, retreating from the spotlight to let God be God and to let Ahaz be Ahaz. He simply waits patiently on the Lord. Solicit opinions of this strategy from the group. Our Lord honors those who humbly wait for Him to act on their behalf. Just as Isa-

iah is content to wait for the Lord, whose way of fulfilling His word of promise is sometimes hidden even to those who know and trust Him, so we, too, wait for our Lord's second coming. We do not know the day or the hour, yet we quietly and peaceably go about our business, confident in the knowledge of our God's sure Word.

13. (a) They sought out witchcraft and mediums. Sadly, like many today, they looked for a way to connect to power outside themselves, a power beyond the technology that is doomed to fail in any age, no matter how sophisticated that society's science. Despite their own failing power, they refused to turn and heed the Word of God. (b) The result was darkness, distress, and despair. And, of course, they blamed everyone else, even their king and their God. (c) The passage from Revelation echoes the same sinful stubbornness, the same sinful arrogance that lies resident in hearts that refuse to repent and believe the Gospel. The consequences for sin always fall on someone else's shoulders. Those who pull their doom down around their own ears by their own actions always want to find a scapegoat, someone besides themselves to blame for what happens to them. So Judah did. So sinners will continue to do until eternity invades time.

Day 5 • Isaiah 9:1–7

14. Point out that as the northernmost tribes, Zebulun and Naphtali were the first to feel the effects of foreign invasion. They lay on Israel's periphery and thus in closer contact with the nations of the Gentiles. To the political and religious elite in Jerusalem, especially at the time of Christ, Galilee was clearly a second-rate place to live. But as Isaiah's great prophesy points out, the first to feel the gloom would be the first to find the gladness! Isaiah speaks of a great light coming. The ministry of Jesus began in the darkness of remote Galilee. From there He moved toward the seat of Davidic power, bringing His ministry to culmination in Jerusalem where He enters as His people's humble King.

15. Answers will vary. Participants may mention such things as the joy and new meaning of life they find in Jesus.

16. (a) Point out that the word *wonderful* in Hebrew carries with it the sense of miraculous wonder. The word *counselor* frequently referred to a human advisor who counseled royalty. While many human kings might be described as "mighty," the Messiah would be "Mighty God." Ancient peoples often called their rulers "Father"; the Messiah, however, would be an "Everlasting Father." Other princes came and went, but only the Messiah would be the "Prince of Peace" who would bring true peace to His people. Although other kings would follow Ahaz in the Davidic line, none would fully fit Isaiah's magnificent description of the Messiah until Jesus came. Jesus was the very Son of God, David's Son and David's Lord. (b) *For personal reflection. Sharing optional.* Answers will vary. Ask volunteers to share as time will allow.

His Hand Is Stretched Out Still

Isaiah 9:8–12:6

Preparing for the Session

Central Focus

God's hand is stretched out in judgment on all who rebel against Him. God's hand of judgment fell fully on Christ Jesus, the Prince of Peace, great David's greater Son, who hung on the cross and absorbed all of God's wrath against human sin. As we look forward to the coming of that Kingdom in all its fullness, we continue to spread the Good News of that Kingdom so that our God's great name may be known on all the earth.

Objectives

That the participant, led by the Holy Spirit through the Word, will

1. better understand God's justice and mercy, especially as the two can be described in the words "His hand is stretched out still";
2. see himself or herself as among the remnant, the believing saints whom God has delivered from judgment and restored as citizens of the Messiah's peaceful kingdom; and
3. trust more deeply in the God who is our strength, song, and salvation.

For the Small-Group Leader

Small-Group Discussion Helps

Day 1 • Isaiah 9:8–10:4

1. (a) Answers will vary depending upon the Bible translation the participants have used. Have one or two different versions read aloud. (b) Again, answers will vary. The pertinent phrase in the ESV is "His anger has not turned away, and His hand is stretched out still." (c) The words "His hand is stretched out still" carry a double meaning. God's hand of judgment is about to fall, but it has not yet fallen. God is still allowing His people time to repent. This possibility and our knowledge that God receives and forgives penitent sinners gives us hope.

2. Focus on the arrogance of human beings, especially the arrogance that does not receive God's correction with humble repentance, but plans instead to patch up life in such a way that makes it more comfortable than ever before.

3. Focus on the sins of spiritual leaders who lie about God and His judgment on sin and their listeners' need for repentance and who tolerate or even encourage hypocrisy by their teaching.

4. Depending on what details participants choose to focus on, their responses will vary. The verses paint a picture of fiery anger and judgment, of lovelessness and famine, of infighting and intense family rivalry ("Manasseh devours Ephraim"). The judgment was historically fulfilled at Isaiah's time and will have final fulfillment at the Last Day.

5. This stanza of the song condemns injustice, especially injustice that hurts the poor and helpless, widows and orphans.

6. *For personal reflection. Sharing optional.* (a) Don't expect anyone to answer this question aloud. (b) Ask volunteers to express the comfort they received from the words of Gospel found in Isaiah 12 that are referenced here.

Day 2 • Isaiah 10:5–19

7. Assyria arrogantly took credit for its military victories. The people of that nation assumed they had been able to conquer as much territory as they had because they themselves were wise and strong. In reality, God had given them their victories. He had used them as His tool. Now that the task was done, He would see to it that they received the judgment they deserved for their sin that was no less than Israel's.

8. *For personal reflection. Sharing optional.* You may wish

to ask for comments on what makes taking credit for our own accomplishments so spiritually deadly. If no one mentions it, point out that such actions spring from sinful pride. On the one hand, our Lord does want us to enjoy seeing the results of our efforts. But even as we note what He has done through us, we must never forget that this is exactly what has happened—He has done them through us. This is never more true than when we go about the work of His kingdom. As time will allow, refer participants to Isaiah 26:12. The ESV translation of this verse makes the point abundantly clear.

9. **Challenge question.** Let participants respond. Today's reading contains little comfort. God speaks His Law through the prophet Isaiah in stark, unmistakable terms. Verses 5–6 show God in control of world events for the sake of His Church.

Day 3 • Isaiah 10:20–34

10. (a) Let a few volunteers share their responses. Some may refer to fabric remnants or to other materials left over during the manufacturing process. Accept reasonable responses. (b) Israel's remnant included all those who would return to the Lord in repentance and faith. It also includes all God's saints of all time and place who have responded to His love in repentance and faith. Make sure everyone in your group understands that both repentance and faith come to us not as we try to drum them up inside ourselves, but as God's gift to us (see also Romans 2:4 and Ephesians 2:8–9). (c) Let participants comment. In one sense, the idea of a remnant returning would seem discouraging because it meant that only a few would be saved. On the other hand, a few would indeed be saved. They would not be wiped out completely. God had not forgotten His promise to send a Savior through the line of David. He would keep that promise.

11. *For personal reflection. Sharing optional.* (a) Ask volunteers to talk about this question in general terms. We most likely rely on those who only hurt us any time we expect people to do for us what God alone can do. If no one mentions it, suggest that sometimes we "lean on [those] who [strike us]" by trusting in ourselves. We're often our own worst enemies because we insist on taking our lives into our own hands instead of leaving them in the faithful hands of our Lord. (b) Point participants to the Word of God and to the Sacraments as the sources of the strength they need to "lean on the LORD, the Holy One of Israel."

Day 4 • Isaiah 11

12. (a) Ask for individual responses. Sin in the lives of others and the sin in our own hearts lie at the center of all our peace deficits. (b) These texts refer to the spiritually poor, who are in need of the riches of Christ's mercy, and to the spiritually meek, who humbly look to Christ for the goodness and righteousness that is missing in their own hearts. Note Jesus' words in Matthew 5:3–5: "Blessed are the poor in spirit." (c) The Prince of Peace will judge the poor with righteousness. It's critical to note that He gives us His own righteousness. He can do this because He has taken our punishment (see also 2 Corinthians 5:21). This is very good news indeed!

13. (a) Let volunteers read some of their answers. (b) Nineteenth-century evolutionists painted a grim picture of "nature red in tooth and claw." In these verses, Isaiah portrays animals that are natural enemies coexisting peacefully. His extended description symbolizes the kind of peace of heart and mind that the Messiah will bring in its fullness when He "has put all things [including death] in subjection under His feet" (1 Corinthians 15:27). We experience this peace even now as we look forward to our heavenly home. (c) *For personal reflection. Sharing optional.* Do not ask for specific responses. Do, however, point to the fact that we need not wait for Christ's peaceful kingdom until we go to live with our Lord in our heavenly home. We enjoy that peace right now. (d) We wait for the time when Christ comes in His glory to judge the world and to take His people home with Him forever.

Day 5 • Isaiah 12

14. (a) Many of the same thoughts recur in all three hymns, as do many of the same words and phrases. Most notable among these are the words from Exodus and Isaiah, "the LORD GOD is my strength and my song, and He has become my salvation." All three reflect a concern that God's glory be declared among all peoples and nations on the earth. All three exalt God for His greatness. (b) **Challenge question.** Let participants com-

ment. Accept reasonable responses. We may, for example, conclude that God's people have always looked to Him for the same things and have always found Him faithful to provide what He has promised—salvation, deliverance, hope, and forgiveness. God's people have always worshiped Him for His majesty, mercy, greatness, and glory. We will worship Him for those same attributes throughout eternity. These similarities point out the unity of the Church and the "communion of saints," as the Apostles' Creed calls it, throughout all time and place and even into eternity itself.

15. *For personal reflection. Sharing optional.* Let volunteers offer suggestions.

Fallen Is Babylon the Great

Isaiah 13–17

Preparing for the Session

Central Focus

These chapters begin what Bible scholars have called the Gentile oracles. In the texts for this week, God condemns the Gentile nations for their rebellion and stubborn pride. Even as our Lord does that, He comforts His people with the promise that their oppression under these nations will soon come to an end.

But the Lord also has another purpose in mind for these acrid declarations of His judgment. As He confronts the nations with their sin, He also desires to lead them to repentance and faith in the Savior who is to come.

Objectives

That the participant, led by the Holy Spirit through the Word, will

1. understand Babylon as the world system that throughout history has set itself against God and against His Christ;
2. take comfort in the ultimate defeat of this world system;
3. recognize that by God's act of claiming us in Baptism we are a people distinct and different from the nations;
4. use the Holy Spirit's power to resist the influences of the world, the devil, and his or her own flesh.

For the Small-Group Leader

Small-Group Discussion Helps

Day 1 • Isaiah 13

1. (a) Answers will vary. Ask several volunteers to read theirs. In these verses, God is calling His armies together, rallying them for war. (b) The "day of the LORD" will be horrible, filled with fear, pain, death, and destruction. (c) For instance, Isaiah 13:19–22 says, "Babylon . . . will be like Sodom and Gomorrah when God overthrew them. . . . It will never be inhabited or lived in for all generations . . . no Arab will pitch his tent there . . . no shepherds will make their flocks lie down there. But wild animals will lie down there . . . there ostriches will dwell, and there wild goats will dance. Hyenas will cry in its towers, and jackals in the pleasant palaces."

2. **Challenge question.** The description of "the day of the LORD" given in Isaiah 13:10 sounds much like that of the prophet Joel and of Jesus Himself as they prophesied about Judgment Day. The shaking of heaven and earth (v. 13) corresponds closely to the description given in Hebrews 12:26 of the Last Day. In Isaiah 13:11, God threatens to punish the world for its wickedness. For all these reasons, we may conclude that God is not here addressing ancient Babylonia exclusively, but also anyone who would identify with the powers of this world.

3. The people of Babel banded together in their rebellion against God and their refusal to worship Him. In pride, they chose instead to build a city and a tower. God had commanded that human beings fill the earth. Instead, these people decided to stick together in the plain of Shinar. God scattered them by confusing their languages. This plain later became the geographic center of the Babylonian Empire.

4. Sometimes when we see the wickedness of the world around us and especially when we face persecution, ridicule, or other opposition because of our faith in Christ, we can become discouraged. But our Lord promises us that evil will not win forever, even though it appears to be winning now. God will call a halt to sin. God will avenge His people. He will punish the wicked even as He comforts His children.

Day 2 • Isaiah 14:1–23

5. (a) Isaiah's taunt song against the king of Babylon tells of the pomp of that king's reign (v. 11), his arrogance (vv. 12–14), his power (vv. 16–17), his lack of

compassion (v. 17), and his heartlessness or immorality (v. 20). Accept other responses the participants can reasonably defend. (b) Both the king of Babylon and Babel's builders sought to elevate themselves to heaven. In pride, they wanted to live as their own ultimate authority, higher in power than God Himself. (c) Babylon's king boasted that he would ascend to heaven, set his throne on high, and sit on the mount of assembly. He would also ascend above the heights of the clouds and would make himself like the Most High. (d) God responded by saying (Isaiah 14:22–23), "I will rise up against them . . . and will cut off from Babylon name and remnant, descendants and posterity . . . I will make it a possession of the hedgehog, and pools of water, and I will sweep it with the broom of destruction."

6. The "man of lawlessness" (called the Antichrist elsewhere in 1 John) speaks in the same boastful, self-aggrandizing way as the king of Babylon and as the original inhabitants of Babel. The rebellion is the same, the opposition to God is the same, the pride is the same, the desire to be god is the same, and—most significantly of all—the destruction is the same.

7. See the answer to question 5. Again in these words God extends hope to those oppressed by what the New Testament calls "the spirit of lawlessness" that is active in our world today, even as it was active at Babel and in the ancient Babylonian Empire. The world-system that sides with Satan and that opposes God and His people will not stand forever. God will call a halt to its power and destruction.

Day 3 • Isaiah 14:1–23

8. (a) God promises to show mercy to His people. He has chosen them as His own. He will not forget or abandon them. (b) Isaiah speaks of sojourners who will join "the house of Jacob." They are non-Jewish or Gentile believers.

9. Let participants name examples. Help the group see that persecution need not involve physical violence. Job discrimination, snide remarks, and the anguish of heart we feel as we see the violence and wickedness of our society all contribute to the oppression and turmoil God's people experience as we confront the world-system Babylon in which we are immersed in this life.

10. *For personal reflection. Sharing optional.* Let volunteers share their thoughts as time will allow.

Day 4 • Isaiah 14:24–16:14

11. (a) Assyria, Philistia, and Moab. (b) Let volunteers offer their opinions.

12. (a) Isaiah 14:32, 15:5, and 16:5 all speak beautifully of God's grace. The picture in 14:32 is one of God establishing Zion, His Church, and those who recognize their spiritual poverty (see also Matthew 5:3) taking refuge there. Isaiah 15:5 says that God's heart cries out over Moab. Even as He judges, God takes no pleasure in the death of the wicked. Finally, Isaiah 16:5 speaks of the Messiah who is to come. This descendent of David will judge in justice and "is swift to do righteousness." In fact, Jesus gives righteousness to all who believe in Him. (b) God is simply not some omnipotent despot, a bully in the sky. Indeed, He will punish the wicked, but He longs for all to turn to Him in repentance and faith so that He may have mercy instead of acting in wrath.

Day 5 • Isaiah 17

13. Damascus (vv. 1, 3) was the capital of Syria (Aram). Ephraim (v. 3) was the leading tribe of the Northern Kingdom. Remind participants of the coalition between the Northern Kingdom and Syria they studied in Isaiah 7. (The Bible sometimes uses Ephraim as a synonym for the Northern Kingdom.)

14. The verses cited would implicate Syria and Ephraim in the sins of idolatry and forgetting (ignoring) the Lord—the Lord who wanted to save them!

15. *For personal reflection. Sharing optional.* Ask volunteers to share any insights they derived from thinking through the questions here as time will permit.

Hope for the Hopeless

Isaiah 18–23

Preparing for the Session

Central Focus

These chapters continue the Gentile oracles. They pronounce God's judgment against still more nations that have rebelled against God and insisted on going their own way. But besides hearing harsh words of Law, we also hear words of comfort and promise through the Messiah who would come.

Objectives

That the participant, led by the Holy Spirit through the Word, will

1. grow in his or her appreciation of the great treasure of salvation opened to us by the Key of David, Jesus, our Savior; and
2. do all he or she can in word and deed to share this precious hope with others.

For the Small-Group Leader

Small-Group Discussion Helps

Day 1 • Isaiah 18

1. (a) He remains quiet and does not act. (b) In verse 5, that judgment is pictured as the pruning process in which sprigs and branches are cut away.

2. **Challenge question.** (a) The Ethiopians will present tribute at Mount Zion, "the place of the name of the LORD of hosts." In other words, they will bring offerings to the Lord, a sign that they believe in and worship Him. (b) The Ethiopian eunuch, through the preaching of Isaiah, became a follower of Jesus. According to Church history, he returned to his homeland and spread the Gospel there. To this day there is an active Christian Church in Ethiopia. This Gentile nation belongs to Zion!

3. God cared enough about the Gentile nations to warn them of their sin and of its results. He then told them how to escape judgment for their wrongdoing, and He promised a Savior, the Messiah who would die for the sins of the world.

Day 2 • Isaiah 19–20

4. Accept reasonable responses. The pronouncements of judgment are hard to listen to because of their severity and also because we see ourselves as deserving the same kind of punishment that Isaiah warned the pagan nations about.

5. How often we fail to consult God's Word and pray in time of need! While there's nothing wrong with seeing a doctor when we are sick or getting the best advice we can when we buy a house or look for a job, there is something seriously wrong if we fail to seek God's wisdom and pray for His intervention on our behalf. It's also wrong if we follow advice we know to be sinful or deceitful (e.g., lying about our experience on a resume or falsifying our income tax return). Behind a sinful action, a sinful attitude can always be found—a lack of trust in our Lord to provide adequately for us (greed or worry).

6. (a) Let volunteers share responses. (b) The Lord Almighty will bless them, saying, "Blessed be Egypt My people, and Assyria the work of My hands, and Israel My inheritance." (c) The personal pronoun (My) stresses God's involvement with each individual on earth, regardless of his or her nationality. Our Lord has revealed Himself as a jealous God (Exodus 20:5), fiercely committed to us and protective of us, insistent that we look to Him and to Him alone as the source of all good.

7. (a) That Egypt and Cush (Ethiopia) would be humbled and disgraced when the Assyrians took captive their people, as they had the inhabitants of Philistine Ashdod. As the reference in 2 Chronicles indicates, such stripping of captives was a common practice to gain both the clothes as booty and to humble and shame a defeated enemy. (b) It was intended to warn them not to rely on Egypt and Cush.

Day 3 • Isaiah 21

8. (a) "Fallen, fallen is Babylon; and all the carved images of her gods he has shattered to the ground" (v. 9b). "Morning comes, and also the night. If you will inquire, inquire; come back again" (v. 12). (b) The second watchman seems unconcerned. Apparently judgment had not come for Dumah. He does not seem prepared for when judgment will arrive.

9. **Challenge question.** Many participants will likely name their pastor, parents, teachers, and even special fellow believers for that role. The language of Hebrews 13:17 supports this response: "Obey your leaders and submit to them, for they are keeping watch over your souls, as those who will have to give an account. Let them do this with joy and not with groaning, for that would be of no advantage to you." Allow individuals to keep their thoughts to themselves about how likely they are to listen to the watchmen in their lives, but do accept suggestions as to how God's people might show thankfulness for the blessings that come to them from God through their pastor and other spiritual mentors.

Day 4 • Isaiah 22

10. (a) Verse 2—Worldly merrymaking. Verse 3—The leaders will flee. Verses 6–7—Overwhelming military force by the enemy. (Note: Elamites probably fought in the Babylonian army. Kir is probably another name for Media.) (b) Jerusalem will fall because God has removed His protecting hand (v. 8). He has done this because, although the citizens of Judah did all they could humanly do to protect themselves (vv. 9–11a), they had not taken the spiritual remedies God had continually demanded through His prophets. They had not looked to Him for hope and help. They had not repented of their sins. Instead, they had lived in decadence and hedonism, saying to each other, "Let us eat and drink, for tomorrow we die" (v. 13). Verse 14—No repentance results in no atonement.

11. (a) Shebna occupied himself with building an elaborate tomb or sepulcher in which he planned to be buried, indicating his self-interest and pride. (b) Eliakim would serve his people responsibly and in faithfulness. (c) Eliakim was God's servant, just as was Christ. He served his people selflessly and in compassion, just as would Christ. He would seek his people's good, rather than his own. In all these ways, Eliakim was like the coming Messiah.

12. Let volunteers share their thoughts.

Day 5 • Isaiah 23

13. Let participants share responses. Likely, people will report fear, even terror. Some may suggest indifference, and this answer is a valid one too, for that's just how the people of Tyre reacted (or rather, did not act).

14. *For personal reflection. Sharing optional.* You might ask volunteers to comment on any insights they gained as a result of thinking this through.

In That Day

Isaiah 24–27

Preparing for the Session

Central Focus

Our Savior has defeated Satan and swallowed up the death we deserved because of our sin by absorbing the wrath of God in our place. He has planted us in His Church and enables us to bear abundant fruit. We praise Him now and into eternity.

Objectives

That the participant, led by the Holy Spirit through the Word, will

1. praise God for His victory over sin, Satan, and death;
2. bear abundant fruit, confident in the righteousness already his or hers in Christ; and
3. look forward with eagerness to the day in which Christ will come in all His glory to gather His people to live with Him forever.

For the Small-Group Leader

Small-Group Discussion Helps

Day 1 • Isaiah 24:1–25:5

1. (a) The judgments in today's readings differ from the Gentile oracles in that judgment falls on the entire earth and all its people (v. 6); the physical planet will be destroyed (v. 19), see also 2 Peter 3:10; the destruction is an eternal one (v. 20b); God will punish (v. 21) the host of exalted ones "in heaven" (Satan and his angels) but also the kings of the earth (earthly rulers and their followers); and God will establish His final, eternal, perfect rule (24:23–25:5). (b) Answers will vary. Accept responses based on the text. (c) Again, answers will vary.

2. Give participants time to share the words they chose and the reasons they chose the phrases they did.

Day 2 • Isaiah 25:6–12

3. Answers will vary. Affirm those based in the text (e.g., "Praise God for Death's Destruction").

4. God's great banquet features are sumptuous food (v. 6), choice wine (v. 6), total joy (vv. 8–9), and an absence of shame (v. 8).

5. Perhaps the most important additional detail included in the New Testament readings referenced here is the fact that the banquet celebrates the marriage of the Lamb. It's the feast God gives in celebration of His Son's wedding. We—the Church—are His bride. We are His honored guests. Only in Christ and because of Christ can we attend this banquet. Only in Christ and because of Christ have hell, sin, and death been swallowed up for us. (See also 1 Corinthians 15:51–57)

6. Let participants share their thoughts. In the Holy Supper we receive the most nourishing, most joy-producing food and drink of all—Christ's holy body and precious blood. These are the very elements whereby He earned salvation for us and through which He has destroyed the power of hell, sin, death, and Satan forever.

7. Lead participants to personalize and to express the truth "Jesus died for me." Be alert to the special needs of any non-Christians in the group. Be ready to personally witness to them of your faith in Christ and to pray for them, that the Spirit may indeed lead them to faith in Christ.

Day 3 • Isaiah 26:1–11

8. As with the earlier questions that asked for titles, accept reasonable responses. Ask several volunteers to share their thoughts as time will allow.

9. The city here, as elsewhere in Isaiah, refers to Zion or Jerusalem and here foresees the restoration of the city and nation as the people of Israel return from exile.

But especially, as the cross references indicate, the city refers to heaven. "In that day" (v. 1) is the day of final victory when God's enemies will experience judgment and God's people will experience the ultimate joy of their Lord in the new Jerusalem, in the heaven He has prepared for them.

10. Because Jesus took our sin, God has imputed Christ's righteousness—His right standing before the Father—to us. When God looks at us, He sees Jesus' holiness and Jesus' faithfulness. What an awesome concept, especially for those of us who are painfully aware of our sin and our unfaithful words and actions.

11. (a) God keeps us in His peace—note that it's His action—as we look to Him for help and strength. When we ignore His promises and neglect His Word, we lapse into fear, doubt, confusion, and perhaps even panic. (b) Don't force anyone to answer this question. Share yourself, if you can do that in comfort. Then ask for volunteers. (c) Since looking to ourselves or to any human source for help and strength in times of need constitutes sin, we need to confess our worries, and restless lack of peace, to our Lord. We know on the basis of His promises (e.g., 1 John 1:8–9) that He will forgive us and in His gracious absolution also empower us to live more trustfully, more peacefully. Other possible answers include personal or group prayer, singing praises to God, and devotional reading

12. **Challenge question.** Those who reject mercy will receive justice. God's holiness demands it. And insofar as we are released from the misery our enemies have caused, we rejoice. So rejoicing in the destruction of Satan and his allies is not somehow unloving or unchristian. However, Christ encourages us to focus on the greatest source of joy: our salvation. God does truly want all to be saved and to come to the knowledge of the truth. In Jesus, He has made a way for every human being to receive forgiveness and the gift of eternal life.

Day 4 • Isaiah 26:12–21

13. Verse 12—Both parts of this verse credit God with His work in the lives of His people: "Lord, You will ordain peace for us," and "You have done for us all our works." Verse 14—The phrases in this verse that point out the hopelessness of finding salvation apart from the Lord include the words that emphasize human mortality (e.g., "They are dead," "They will not live," "They will not arise," You "wiped out all remembrance of them.") Verses 17–18—"We have given birth to wind," "We have accomplished no deliverance in the earth," "The inhabitants of the world have not fallen." All this occurred despite our labor and despite pain so intense it felt like childbirth. These verses kill any hope human beings have that they will, by trying hard and suffering long, bring themselves new life.

14. All masters whom human beings serve will die. All memory of them dissolves (v. 14), but the Lord's dead—or as St. John would put it, "the dead who die in the Lord" (Revelation 14:13)—will live. Their dead bodies will rise from the dust. They will awaken and shout for joy (v. 19).

15. Ask volunteers to share.

Day 5 • Isaiah 27

16. (a) Satan, the ancient serpent, is Leviathan, who invaded Eden and has been stealing, killing, and destroying (John 10:10) on earth ever since. (b) The Lord will punish and slay him "in that day" (the Day of Judgment). The twisted serpent who has caused so much suffering and pain will trouble God's people no longer.

17. **Challenge question.** God tends and protects this vineyard, His Church. His people respond to His love, unlike most in ancient Israel described in the parable found in Isaiah 5. They (we) "blossom and put forth shoots and fill the whole world with fruit" (27:6).

18. These verses also speak forcefully of the day Christians call Good Friday in which God's wrath at our sin fell on our Lord Jesus. By this, our sin was taken away and our guilt atoned for. (Note the similarity in the language here and in Isaiah 6:7.)

19. **Challenge question.** The sounding of the trumpet; God's people being gathered from all places in the world; worship on the holy mountain of Mount Zion in Jerusalem, the holy city, a symbol of heaven. All these are vivid pictures of the coming realities of the Last Day, judgment, resurrection of the body, and heaven.

What Are You Waiting For?

Isaiah 28–30

Preparing for the Session

Central Focus

God's message to ancient Judah, like His message to us, never changes. He urges us to return to Him in repentance and faith so that in Christ He can forgive our sins and give us eternal life. He freely supplies all He demands. Even faith and repentance come to us as a gift. His faithfulness brings us hope and comfort.

Objectives

That the participant, led by the Holy Spirit through the Word, will

1. ask God to show him or her the hardness of heart, the spiritual blindness, that may be keeping him or her from seeing the truths of His Word;
2. cling to Jesus, the lion of Judah and the hearth of God, who endured the wrath of God in his or her place; and
3. look to the Lord as his or her only deliverer and source of peace, especially in times of difficulty.

For the Small-Group Leader

Small-Group Discussion Helps

Day 1 • Isaiah 28

1. (a) Accept reasonable responses. Isaiah preached a message aimed at evoking repentance and faith in the hearts of his listeners. The people were ignoring God and His laws. They neglected worship or at best went through the outward motions of worship without any inward change. They worshiped idols—both the false gods of the nations around them as well as material possessions. They looked to themselves to invent schemes that would bring them security (e.g., political alliances with the nations around them) instead of turning to the only source of true security—their Lord. (b) God promised to forgive and to restore those who returned to Him in repentance and faith. He would heal, protect, save, and deliver them.

2. (a) The message of this week's reading is strikingly similar to the message God had delivered to these same people years before. They had not yet repented or believed. God had no new message for them, even though they may have gotten tired of this one. (b) Accept responses volunteers can justify from the text. (c) Just as God's message of Law and judgment had not changed, neither had His promises. Again, accept responses participants can cite when comparing Isaiah 1–12 with today's reading.

3. *For personal reflection. Sharing optional.* Don't ask anyone to volunteer specifics for (a). Do, however, ask if anyone would like to share his or her thoughts on (b). When we see God's faithfulness to His Old Testament people, faithfulness that kept on reaching out to them despite their sin, we find comfort in knowing that He also remains faithful to us in Jesus Christ. That is one reason New Testament believers can find the Old Testament so helpful. Refer the group to Romans 15:4–6 as time will allow.

4. (a) The stone is Jesus, who is the cornerstone of the Church, all who trust in Him for salvation. (b) In Isaiah's time, now, and until the Day of Judgment, it is people's unbelief that condemns them to judgment. God's forgiveness is there, won by Christ. God yearns to have sinners repent and believe. But many "stumble because they disobey the word" (1 Peter 2:8).

Day 2 • Isaiah 29:1–14

5. **Challenge question.** Because of the people's persistent unbelief and stubborn refusal to repent, Jerusalem became God's hearth at the time Nebuchadnezzar of Babylon invaded Judah and took God's people into captivity. In today's lecture, it will become clear that the hearth imagery extends much further—to Calvary, to our own Baptism, to any time God touches His people

in Word and Sacrament, to the final Day of Judgment. If someone mentions any of this now, acknowledge that they are correct. If not, simply defer discussion of this point until the lecture.

6. (a) When to plant and when to plow; not to keep on plowing, but also to plant and wait for a harvest. (b) God's people won't pay attention when He calls them to repent. (c) The cited references (and others in the Old Testament) use plowing as a picture of repentance. (d) They have closed their eyes to God's truth so often that they have become stupefied as though drunk. They are numb and blind. In fact, everything Isaiah has said to them has become like a closed book presented to someone who is illiterate. They couldn't get God's message even if they wanted to.

7. *For personal reflection. Sharing optional.* Speak God's forgiving word to your group. God Himself promises to open the ears of the deaf and the eyes of the blind. He will fill our hearts with joy—the peace of sins forgiven and fellowship restored.

Day 3 • Isaiah 29:15–24

8. Invite volunteers to share their paraphrases. The point to be made is that the people are acting as though they could hide their sins and their schemes from the Lord—the omniscient one! They have deceived themselves into thinking that He doesn't know what's going on in their lives. How hardened and spiritual blind sin can make us!

9. Compare 29:11–12 with 29:18–19. (a) The vision that has been sealed and unreadable becomes open and intelligible. The message brings great joy as well. (b) This is God's work. For ancient Judah as for us today, repentance comes to us as God's gift. He works it in our hearts through His Word. In that sense, His Law is a wonderful gift to us in that it points out our sin and our need for our Savior.

10. **Challenge question.** The Lord drew Abraham, His people's forefather, out of the darkness of idolatry. He "bought him back" (redeemed him) from bondage to sin and death. In the same way, the Lord wants to bring His people out of their bondage to sin now.

11. (a) God works through His Word and the Sacraments to accomplish this. Invite participants to mention some of the people through whom God's Word comes to them. (b) Let individuals keep their answers to themselves, but do encourage them to thank God for His holy work in their lives. (c) *For personal reflection. Sharing optional.* This prayer should remain between each individual and the Lord.

Day 4 • Isaiah 30:1–17

12. Judah seems determined to form a defensive alliance with Egypt.

13. God had taken His people out of the four hundred years of slavery they suffered in Egypt. His people had spent forty years wandering around in the deserts of the Sinai Peninsula. Now they propose to go back to the sand, heat, and thirst through which they had escaped as God brought them into freedom.

14. (a) The people demanded that Isaiah and God's other prophets stop seeing and hearing from God, that they stop speaking the truth, and instead proclaim what the people wanted to hear, and that they get God out of the way so that the people can get on with living their lives how they want to live them. (b) *For personal reflection. Sharing optional.* Ask if anyone has comments or insights they would like to share based on the questions here. Encourage them to state their observations in general terms rather than feeling they must share specific sins with the group.

15. (a) God brings us to the point that we see our sins as He sees them. He works contrition in our hearts. Then, when we confess our sins, He assures us that He forgives us for Jesus' sake. There simply is no peace like the peace that flows from sins forgiven and from knowing that our fellowship with our heavenly Father has been restored. (b) Let volunteers share as they feel comfortable doing so.

Day 5 • Isaiah 30:18–33

16. Answers may vary somewhat. Accept responses participants can justify from the text. Verse 18—God promises grace and mercy to repentant sinners. Verse 19—God promises to dry the tears of His people and to hear their prayers and their cries for help. Verses 20–21—God promises to direct the steps of His people, to lead them into right (righteous) paths (see also Psalm 5:8).

Verses 23–24—God promises to supply His people's physical needs for food and clothing and to do so in abundance (see also Matthew 6:33). Verses 25–33—God promises to defeat His people's enemies and to give them a "song as in the night" that is continuing joy.

17. Invite volunteers to share their thoughts.

The King in His Beauty

Isaiah 31–33

Preparing for the Session

Central Focus

Israel's true King, Yahweh, is present in the midst of His people. As holy God, He must punish the rebellion and sin of His people. Yet, in His mercy, God seeks to lead His people to repentance and trust in His forgiving love through the Savior He sends.

Objectives

That the participant, led by the Holy Spirit through the Word, will

1. state and explain the five major themes of Isaiah 1–33;
2. think through the implications of these major themes for his or her own life and the life of the Christian Church today;
3. thank God for making him or her part of His Church, His Zion; and
4. live secure in Christ's love, sharing the message of that love with others.

For the Small-Group Leader

Small-Group Discussion Helps

Day 1 • Isaiah 31

1. God urges His people not to rely on the Egyptian alliance because (v. 2a) He is their God and He is wiser than the human wisdom that has devised this alliance; because (v. 2b) He has told them not to do it and "He does not call back His words;" because (v. 3a) the Egyptians are mere human beings and their armaments are human armaments; and because (v. 3b) when the Lord stretches out His hand to act, no human help will accomplish anything, but helper and helpee will both "perish together."

2. **Challenge question.** The incident recorded by Jeremiah illustrates the depth of the spiritual darkness into which those in Judah had fallen. Even after the invasion by Babylon's armies and after Egypt had proven itself an unreliable source of help, the people left in Judah became fearful for their safety. They decided to escape to Egypt. But they wanted their decision blessed, so to speak, by God's spokesman Jeremiah. They asked his advice, already knowing the answer they wanted to hear. Jeremiah confronted them with their unbelief and their rebellion and urged them to stay in Judah. Predictably, they ignored his warnings. In Egypt, they met the destruction and death they had left Judah to escape.

3. (a) Sin blinds us. It is so powerful and insidious and so subtly joins forces with our flesh that any of God's people, no matter how steeped they are in the truths of the faith, can be lulled to sleep by it. (b) *For personal reflection. Sharing optional.* Ask participants to review their responses to this question privately. Give them a moment to do this. Then move into the next question. Do not ask anyone to share responses. (c) *For personal reflection. Sharing optional.* How important it is that we rely not on our own wisdom, but on the wisdom of God! How important that we maintain close ties with other believers who know God's Word and who will tell us the truth about ourselves, even if that truth hurts from time to time. How important that we know and trust the teaching and counsel of our pastor and that we listen to his warnings. And how comforting it is to know that when we do stumble, we can return to the Lord, our God, and find in Him a gracious and merciful Father who will receive us, forgive us, and empower us to throw away our idols, regardless of what they might be.

4. The prophecy and fulfillment of deliverance from the Assyrian enemy was as dramatic and drastic in scope as the Passover deliverance from Egypt. In both cases, God's angel passed over the people and inflicted punishment on the enemy.

Day 2 • Isaiah 32:1–8

5. (a) King Hezekiah is no doubt meant, a king who indeed reigned "in righteousness," as the 2 Kings text indicates. (b) The deeper, ultimate fulfillment is in Christ, the King of righteousness, who was born, lived, and died so that we might receive God's righteousness. (c) Ask participants to share their lists. Accept any justified by the text. For instance, the spiritually blind (Isaiah 32:3) will now see clearly, and the ears once deaf to God's truth will listen and hear. Those who rejected God's Word as mere babbling (28:10, 13) will now hear it speak plainly to them (32:4). Those who foolishly rely on the world's wisdom (32:5) will no longer be considered wise, and the wickedness of their schemes will be revealed for what it is. The deserts and deserted cities (32:12–14) will become a fruitful field (32:15) and God's people, whose lives have been devoid of the fruit of the Spirit (Galatians 5:22–23), will produce love, joy, peace, patience, kindness, goodness, gentleness, faithfulness, and self-control in abundance. Justice and righteous living will be the hallmarks of the lives of those who have accepted their King's gift of righteousness (32:16–17), and these will result in peace and security for themselves and in their relationships. God will destroy His people's enemies (32:19; compare Isaiah 30:30, in which Isaiah uses hail as an image of God's destructive power in Assyria's fall) and will bring the city—His own people, Jerusalem—to true humility before Him.

Day 3 • Isaiah 32:9–20

6. (a) Trust in ourselves is so deadly that God warns against it again and again throughout Scripture. God's people in Judah not only looked to their own foolish human wisdom and religious ritual to carry them through the dangers they faced, they refused even to consider the possibility that these things might fail them. Such complacency led to the destruction of their nation. Spiritual complacency can lead to an even worse fate—eternal death in hell. (b) Let participants comment on the dangers of falling asleep in our faith, of taking our relationship with Christ for granted and drifting away from the Word, from the Sacraments, worship with God's people, prayer, and, eventually, from Christ Himself.

7. Let volunteers suggest some. The words they choose will likely reflect the loneliness and despair of defeat and devastation.

8. Again, let volunteers suggest some. This time the words they choose will reflect the joy and peace of restoration.

9. The difference has come because God's Spirit has been poured out on His people. If time will allow, refer the group back to 11:1–2, which describes the fullness of the Holy Spirit who rested upon the Lord Jesus. Then point the participants to Joel 2:28–31, which talks about the day of Pentecost in vivid detail and was quoted by the apostle Peter on that day (Acts 2:14–36).

10. (a) As you discuss this question, point out that it's no accident that the fruit you talked about earlier (Galatians 5:22–23) is called the fruit of the Spirit. Just as we are justified by God's grace freely as His gift, so we are also sanctified (made more like Christ) freely as God works the needed changes in our hearts. As we keep on confessing our sins and receiving His forgiveness, the Holy Spirit continues to cleanse us from all unrighteousness. The verses of this passage list fruitfulness of life, righteousness, peace, quietness, security, and humility as results of the Holy Spirit's work in the lives of God's people. (b, c) Don't ask anyone to comment on the specific answers they gave to these questions. You might ask about what impact the questions made. Were individuals able to see that God had been at work in their lives, perhaps in ways they had scarcely been aware of? Accept comments as you have time to do so.

Day 4 • Isaiah 33:1–12

11. (a) Isaiah addresses this woe to the destroyer who has not yet been destroyed. He also addresses his words to the traitor who has not yet been betrayed. From outside sources and from the geographic allusions in verse 9, most Bible scholars have concluded that chapter 33 is addressed to Assyria, whose armies pillaged the cities of Judah and ravaged the countryside, but never fully conquered the Southern Kingdom. (b) This woe is good news for God's people because it describes the certain victory that God will win for them.

12. (a) Throughout his Book, Isaiah has painted our Lord as a victorious, delivering, forgiving, and saving

King. This chapter continues to fill in the details of that picture. (b) Let volunteers share their thoughts as time will allow.

Day 5 • Isaiah 33:13–24

13. God calls on all people far and near to hear and to acknowledge what He has done.

14. (a) The "sinners in Zion" may refer to those who lived inside the city walls of Jerusalem during a siege by the Assyrians. In a larger sense, it refers to those who are listed on the books as members of the congregation, but do not really have a living relationship with God or who are by their lifestyle skating very close to the edge. This includes, of course, all of us at times. We all take God's grace for granted sometimes. We all need Christ's gifts of repentance, forgiveness, restoration, and cleansing. Interestingly, Scripture very seldom refers to God's people by the term *sinners*. It does, of course, recognize that we do commit sin and that we will continue to do so until we enter the presence of the Lord in the glories of heaven. But the term *sinner* itself is usually reserved for those outside the faith. In the New Testament, James addresses some harsh words to readers who used God's grace as an excuse to lead lives of sin. He wrote, "Draw near to God, and He will draw near to you. Cleanse your hands, you sinners, and purify your hearts, you double-minded" (James 4:8). We know James was talking to believers because a few verses later (v. 11), he refers to his readers as his brothers. When Isaiah speaks of the "sinners in Zion," he refers to people caught in the same kind of lifestyle James condemns. (b) The judgment of God against sin—ultimately consummated by eternal punishment in hell—is the consuming and everlasting burning.

15. Isaiah 33:15 depicts what the life of a believer is like: a response to the forgiving love of God in Christ. Thus it fits with Ephesians 2:10. It's important that participants see the relationship between faith and works. Works never avail to earn us favor with God. Yet through the sanctifying power of God's Spirit, true faith will result in newness of life.

16. Answers will vary. Note that in Isaiah 33:24, God promises forgiveness for all iniquity. The language in the original Hebrew links this verse with 1:4. The prophet Isaiah ends this part of his book with the same ideas he began it with: God will do what is necessary to remove the heavy burden of human sin from our shoulders and He will bring deliverance and salvation. As New Testament believers, we have an even fuller picture of this salvation. We have seen our Lord Jesus, crucified for our sins and raised again for our justification. We, with all believers of all time, will experience the immeasurable joy pictured so graphically in Revelation 21:1–5.

17. Let volunteers share their thoughts. Today's lecture will treat some of these main points.

18. Again, let volunteers share. Affirm those responses participants can justify from the text.

9780758610218